The Trials of the

A Tale of the Second An

Alex. St. Clair Abrams

Alpha Editions

This edition published in 2024

ISBN : 9789362095374

Design and Setting By
Alpha Editions
www.alphaedis.com
Email - info@alphaedis.com

As per information held with us this book is in Public Domain.
This book is a reproduction of an important historical work. Alpha Editions uses the
best technology to reproduce historical work in the same manner it was first
published to preserve its original nature. Any marks or number seen are left
intentionally to preserve its true form.

Contents

PREFACE.

The plot of this little work was first thought of by the writer in the month of December, 1862, on hearing the story of a soldier from New Orleans, who arrived from Camp Douglas just in time to see his wife die at Jackson, Mississippi. Although the Press of that city made no notice of it, the case presented itself as a fit subject for a literary work. If the picture drawn in the following pages appears exaggerated to our readers, they will at least recognize the moral it contains as truthful.

Trusting that the public will overlook its many defects, the Author yet hopes there will be found in this little book, matter of sufficient interest to while away the idle hour of the reader.

ATLANTA, April 20th, 1864.

CHAPTER FIRST.

THE "CRESCENT CITY"—THE HUSBAND'S DEPARTURE.

Kind reader, have you ever been to New Orleans? If not, we will attempt to describe the metropolis of the Confederate States of America.

New Orleans is situated on the Mississippi river, and is built in the shape of a crescent, from which it derives the appellation of "Crescent City." The inhabitants—that is, the educated class—are universally considered as the most refined and aristocratic members of society on the continent. When we say aristocratic, we do not mean a pretension of superiority above others, but that elegance and etiquette which distinguish the *parvenu* of society, and the vulgar, but wealthy class of citizens with which this country is infested. The ladies of New Orleans are noted for their beauty and refinement, and are certainly, as a general thing, the most accomplished class of females in the South, except the fair reader into whose hands this work may fall.

It was in the month of May, 1861, that our story commences. Secession had been resorted to as the last chance left the South for a preservation of her rights. Fort Sumter, had fallen, and from all parts of the land troops were pouring to meet the threatened invasion of their homes. As history will record, New Orleans was not idle in those days of excitement. Thousands of her sons came forward at the first call, and offered their services for the good of the common cause, and for weeks the city was one scene of excitement from the departure of the different companies to Virginia.

Among the thousands who replied to the first call of their country, was Alfred Wentworth, the confidential clerk of one of the largest commission houses in the city. He was of respectable family, and held a high position in society, both on account of his respectability and the elevated talent he had displayed during his career in the world. He had been married for about five years, and two little children—one a light-eyed girl of four summers, and the other an infant of two years—were the small family with which heaven had blessed him.

After joining a company of infantry, and signing the muster roll, Alfred returned home to his wife and informed her of what he had done, expecting that she would regret it. But the patriotic heart of his wife would not reproach him for having performed his duty; so heaving a sigh as she looked at the child in her arms, and the little girl on her fathers knee, a tear trickled down her flushed cheek as she bade him God-speed. The time that elapsed between his enlistment and departure for the seat of war, was spent by Alfred Wentworth in providing a home for his family, so that in the event of his being killed in battle, they should not want. Purchasing a small residence on

Prytania street, he removed his family into it and concluded his business in time for his departure.

The morning of the twenty-second of May broke brightly over the far-famed "Crescent City." Crowds of citizens were seen congregating on Canal street to witness the departure of two more regiments of Orleanians. The two regiments were drawn up in line between Camp and Carondelet streets, and their fine uniforms, glistening muskets and soldierly appearance created a feeling of pride among the people. They were composed principally of Creoles and Americans, proper. The handsome, though dark complexions of the Creoles could be seen lit up with enthusiasm, in conversation with the dark-eyed Creole beauties of the city, while the light-haired and fair-faced sons of the Crescent City were seen mingling among the crowd of anxious relatives who thronged to bid them farewell.

Apart from the mass of volunteers—who had previously stacked their arms—Alfred Wentworth and his wife were bidding that agonizing farewell, which only those who have parted from loved one can feel. His little bright-eyed daughter was clasped in his arms, and every minute he would stoop over his infant and kiss its tiny cheeks. Marks of tears were on the eyelids of his wife, but she strove to hide them, and smiled at every remark made by her daughter. They were alone from the eyes of a curious crowd. Each person present had too much of his own acquaintances to bid farewell, to notice the speechless farewell which the soldier gave his wife. With one arm clasped around her, and the other holding his daughter, Alfred Wentworth gazed long and earnestly at the features of his wife and children, as if to impress the features of those loved ones still firmer in his mind.

"Attention, battalion!" rang along the line in stentorian tones, and the voices of the company officers calling "fall in, boys, fall in!" were heard in the streets. Clasping his wife to his heart, and imprinting a fond, fond kiss of love upon her cheeks, and embracing his children, the soldier took his place in the ranks, and after the necessary commands, the volunteers moved forward. A crowd of their relatives followed them to the depot of the New Orleans, Jackson and Great Northern Railroad, and remained until the cars were out of sight. After the troops had entered, and the train was slowly moving off, one of the soldiers jumped from the platform, and, embracing a lady who stood near, exclaimed:

"Farewell, dearest Eva! God bless you and the children—we shall meet again." As soon as he spoke, Alfred Wentworth sprang into the cars again and was soon swiftly borne from the city.

Mrs. Wentworth remained standing where her husband had left her, until the vast crowd had dispersed, and nothing could be seen of the train but a thin wreath of smoke emerging from the tree-tops in the distance. Calling the colored nurse, who had followed with the children, she bade her return home, and accompanied her back to her now lonely residence.

CHAPTER SECOND.

THE WIFE AND CHILDREN—A VISITOR

The weeks passed slowly to Mrs. Wentworth from the departure of her husband; but her consciousness that he was performing his duty to his country, and the letters he wrote from Virginia, cheered her spirits, and, in a measure, made her forget his absence.

She was alone one evening with her children, who had become the sole treasures of her heart, and on whom she lavished every attention possible, when the ringing of the bell notified her of the presence of a visitor. Calling the servant, she bade her admit the person at the door. The negro left the room to do her mistress' bidding, and shortly after, a handsome gentleman of about thirty-five years of age entered.

"Good morning, Mrs. Wentworth," he said, on entering the room. "I trust yourself and children are in good health."

Mrs. Wentworth rose from her chair, and, slightly inclining her head, replied: "To what circumstance am I indebted for the honor of this visit, Mr. Awtry?"

"Nothing very particular, madam," he replied; "but hearing of your husband's departure, I thought I should lake the liberty of paying a visit to an old acquaintance, and of offering my services, if you should ever need them."

"I thank you for your kindness; and should I *ever* need your services, you may depend upon my availing myself of your offer; although," she added, "I do not think it likely I shall stand in need of any assistance."

"I rejoice to hear it, my dear madam," he replied; "but I trust," he continued, on noticing the look of surprise which covered her features, "that you will not think my offer in the least insulting; for I can assure you, it was only prompted by the most friendly motives, and the recollections of past days."

Mrs. Wentworth made no reply, and he continued: "I hope that, after an absence of five years, the memory of the past has been banished from you. With me things have changed materially. The follies of my youth have, I trust, been expiated, and I am a different man now to what I was when I last saw you."

"Mr. Awtry," replied Mrs. Wentworth, "I feel rather surprised that, after your presence in New Orleans for so many months, you should not have thought proper to renew our acquaintance until after the departure of my husband."

"Pardon me," he quickly answered. "I was introduced to your husband by a mutual friend; and as he never thought proper to extend an invitation to me, I did not think myself authorized to call here. Learning of his departure this morning, and knowing that his circumstances were not of so favorable a character as he could wish, I thought you might pardon my presumption in calling on you when you learned the motive which actuated this visit— believe me, I am sincere; and now," he continued, "will you accept my proffered hand of friendship, and believe that my desire is only to aid the relatives of one of the gallant men who have gone to struggle for their rights?"

Mrs. Wentworth paused a moment before she accepted the extended hand, while her brow appeared clouded. At length, holding out her hand to him, she said:

"I accept your offered friendship, Mr. Awtry, in the same spirit, as I hope, it is given; but, at the same time, trust you shall never be troubled with any importunities from me."

"Thank you—thank you," he replied eagerly; "I shall not prove otherwise than worthy of your friendship. These are your children?" he continued, changing the conversation.

"Yes," she replied, with a look of pride upon her little daughter and the sleeping infant on the sofa; "these are my little family."

Mr. Awtry took the little girl upon his knees and commenced caressing it, and, after remaining for a few moments in unimportant conversation, took his departure with the promise to call at some future time.

As soon as he left Mrs. Wentworth sat down, and resting her hands on the table, spoke to herself on the visit she had received. "What could have induced him to pay me this visit?" she said, musingly; "it is strange—very strange that he should choose this particular time to renew our acquaintance! He spoke honestly, however, and may be sincere in his offers of assistance, should I ever need anything. He is wealthy, and can certainly aid me." She sat there musing, until the little girl, coming up to her, twined her tiny arms round her mother's neck, and asked if it was not time to light the gas.

"Yes, darling," said Mrs. Wentworth, kissing her fondly; "call Betsy and let her get a light."

After the negro had lit the gas, Mrs. Wentworth said to her, "Should that gentleman, who was here to-day, call at any time again, let me know before you admit him."

"Yes, mistis," replied the negro with a curtsey.

CHAPTER THIRD.

MR. HORACE AWTRY.

Mr. Horace Awtry was a native of the State of New York, and was, at the time of writing, about thirty-live years of age. He was a tall and well-formed man, with light hair clustering in curls on a broad and noble looking forehead; his features were well chiselled, and his upper lip was ornamented with a mustache of the same color as his hair. Notwithstanding his handsome features and extravagant display of dress, there was an expression in his dark blue eyes, which, though likely to captivate the young and innocent portion of the fair sex, was not deemed elegant by those who are accustomed to read the features of man. He was very wealthy, but was a perfect type of the *roue*, although a good education and remarkable control of himself rendered it difficult for his acquaintances to charge him with dissipation, or any conduct unworthy of ft gentleman. As this gentleman will occupy a somewhat conspicuous position in our tale, we deem it necessary to go into these particulars.

Some seven years previous to her marriage, and while yet a child, Mrs. Wentworth, with her father, the only surviving relative she had, spent the summer at Saratoga Springs in the State of New York, and there met Mr. Awtry, who was then a handsome and dashing young man. Struck by her beauty, and various accomplishments, he lost no time in making her acquaintance, and before her departure from the Springs, offered her his hand. To his utter astonishment, the proposal was rejected, with the statement that she was already engaged to a gentleman of New Orleans. This refusal would have satisfied any other person, but Horace Awtry was not a man to yield so easily; he, therefore, followed her to New Orleans on her return, and endeavored, by every means in his power, to supplant Alfred Wentworth in the affections of Eva Seymour—Mrs. Wentworth's maiden name—and in the confidence of her father. Failing in this, and having the mortification of seeing them married, he set to work and succeeded in ruining Mr. Seymour in business, which accounts for the moderate circumstances in which we find Mrs. Wentworth and her husband at the commencement of this book. Worn out by his failure in business and loss of fortune, Mr. Seymour died shortly after his daughter's marriage, without knowing who caused his misfortunes, and Horace Awtry returned to the North. After being absent for several years, he came back to New Orleans some months before the departure of Mrs. Wentworth's husband, but never called upon her until after he had left, when she was surprised at the visit narrated in the foregoing chapter.

This gentleman was seated in the portico of the St. Charles Hotel a few mornings after his visit to Mrs. Wentworth, and by his movements of impatience was evidently awaiting the arrival of some one. At last a young man ran down the steps leading from the apartments, and he rose hurriedly to meet him.

"You are the very man I have been waiting to see," said Horace Awtry; "you must excuse my apparent neglect in not calling on you before."

"Certainly, my dear fellow," replied the gentleman. "I am certain your reasons are good for not attending to your arrangement punctually—by the way," he continued, "who the deuce was that lady I saw you escorting to church last Sunday?"

"An acquaintance of mine that I had not seen for years, until a few days ago chance threw me in her path and I paid her a visit."

"Ha, ha, ha," laughed his companion. "I understand; but who is she, and her name? She is very pretty," he continued, gravely.

"Hush, Charlie!" replied Horace; "come to my room in the St. Louis Hotel, and I will tell you all about it."

"Wait a moment, my friend, and let me get some breakfast," he replied.

"Pooh!" said Horace, "we can have breakfast at Galpin's after I have conversed with you at my room; or," he continued, "I will order a breakfast and champagne to be brought up to my room."

"As you like," said the other, taking a couple of cigars from his pocket and offering one to his companion.

After lighting their cigars, the two men left the hotel, and purchasing the New York *Herald* and *News* from the news-dealer below, proceeded to the St. Louis Hotel, where Horace ordered a breakfast and champagne for himself and guest.

Throwing himself on one of the richly-covered couches that ornamented the apartment, Charles Bell—for that was the name of the gentleman—requested his friend to inform him who the lady was that he escorted to church.

"Well, my dear friend," said Horace, "as you appear so desirous to know I will tell you. I met that lady some seven years ago at Saratoga Springs. If she is now beautiful she was ten times so then, and I endeavored to gain her affections. She was, however, engaged to another young man of this city, and on my offering her my hand in marriage, declined it on that ground. I followed her here with the intention of supplanting her lover in her affections, but it was of no avail; they were married, and the only satisfaction

I could find was to ruin her father, which I did, and he died shortly after without a dollar to his name."

"So she is married?" interrupted his companion.

"Yes, and has two children," replied Horace.

"Where is her husband?"

"He left for Virginia some time ago, where I sincerely trust he will get a bullet through his heart," was the very charitable rejoinder.

"What! do you desire to marry his widow?" asked his friend.

"No, indeed," he replied; "but you see they are not in very good circumstances, and if he were once dead she would be compelled to work for a living, as they have no relatives in this State, and only a few in Baltimore. To gain my object, I should pretend that I desired to befriend her—send the two children to some nurse, and then have her all to myself. This," continued the villain, "is the object with which I have called upon her"—

"And paid a visit to church for the first time in your life," said Bell, laughing; "but," he resumed, "it is not necessary for you to wish the husband dead— why not proceed to work at once?"

"Well, so I would, but she is so very particular, that on the slightest suspicion she would take the alarm and communicate to her husband the fact of my having renewed my acquaintance with her, which would, perhaps, bring him home on furlough."

"Nonsense," replied his friend, "the secessionists need every man to assist them in driving back McDowell, and there is no chance of any furloughs being granted; besides which, we are on the eve of a great battle, and for any of the men to ask for a furlough would lay him open to the charge of cowardice."

"That may be all true," said Horace, "but I shall not venture on anything more as yet. As far as I have gone, she believes me actuated by no other motives than the remembrance of my former affection for her, and, with that belief, places implicit trust in me."

The conversation was here interrupted by the appearance of two waiters, one carrying a waiter filled with different descriptions of food, and the other a small basket containing six bottles of champagne. After setting them on a table, Horace inquired what the charges were.

"Twelve dollars, sah," was the reply.

Horace took out his pocket book, and throwing the man a twenty dollar gold piece, told him to pay for the breakfast and champagne, and purchase cigars with the remainder.

The negroes having left, Horace Awtry and his friend proceeded to discuss their breakfast and champagne. After eating for a few minutes in silence, Horace suddenly said:

"Charlie, what do you think of this war?"

"My opinion is, that the South has got in a pretty bad dilemma," replied that gentleman.

"That is identically my impression, but for heaven's sake do not let any one hear you say so. The people are half crazed with excitement, and the slightest word in favor of the North may lay you at the mercy of an infuriated mob."

"What do you intend doing, now the ports are blockaded, and no one can leave the country?" asked his friend.

"Why, remain here and pretend all the friendship possible for the South. Maybe I will get a contract or two, which will further the design of covering my opinions on this contest."

"Such was my idea, but I am afraid that the secesh government will issue their cotton bonds until all the gold is driven from the States, and then we will have nothing but their worthless paper money," replied Bell.

"I have thought of that, and made up my mind to convert all the property I have here into gold at once, which will give me between sixty and seventy thousand dollars, and as fast as I make any of the bonds from contracts, I will sell them for whatever gold they will bring."

"That's a capital idea, my dear follow," said Bell, rising from his chair and slapping Awtry on the shoulder; "I think I shall follow your plan."

The cigars having been brought in, after a few minutes of unimportant conversation, Charles Bell left his friend, with the arrangement to meet at the Varieties theatre in the evening, and Horace Awtry, divesting himself of his clothing, retired to sleep until the evening should come.

CHAPTER FOURTH.

A POLITIC STROKE—THE TELEGRAPHIC DISPATCH.

June and half of July had sped swiftly away. The great battle, which everybody daily expected, had been fought, and the Yankee army ignominiously defeated. As every one of our readers are well acquainted with this battle, I shall not go into any details; enough; as history will tell, to know that it resulted in a glorious victory to the Confederate army, and covered the gallant Southerners with honor.

On the arrival of dispatches giving an account of this victory, to use a vulgar phrase, New Orleans "ran wild." The excitement and exultation of the people were beyond description, and during the same night that the news was received, one scene of gayety was observed in the city. There was one heart, however, that did not share the joy and merriment so universal among the people. In the privacy of her dwelling, with her two children near by, Mrs. Wentworth spent a night of prayer and anxiety, and next morning rose from her bed with the same feeling of anxiety to know whether her husband had escaped unhurt. At about ten o'clock in the morning, a knock was heard at the door, and soon after Mr. Awtry entered.

"How are you this morning, Mrs. Wentworth?" he said, taking her little daughter in his arms and kissing her; "so we have gained a great victory in Virginia."

"Yes," she replied; "but I do feel so anxious to know if my husband is safe."

"Do not think for a moment otherwise," he answered; "why a soldier's wife should not show half as much solicitude as you do."

"I am, indeed, very desirous of knowing his fate and I am sure the fact of being a soldier's wife does not prevent my feeling a desire to ascertain if he is unhurt, or if he is"—she paused at the thought which seemed so horrid in her imagination, and lowering her face in her hands, burst into tears.

"Mother, what are you crying for?" asked her little daughter, who was sitting on Mr. Awtry's knees.

"My dear madam," said Mr. Awtry, "why do you give way to tears? If you desire," he continued, "I will telegraph to Virginia and learn if your husband is safe."

"Thank you—thank you!" she answered eagerly; "I shall feel deeply obligated if you will."

"I shall go down to the telegraph office at once," he said, rising from his seat and placing the child down; "and now, my little darling," he continued, speaking to the child, "you must tell your ma not to cry so much." With these words he shook Mrs. Wentworth's hand and left the house.

The day passed wearily for Mrs. Wentworth; every hour she would open one of the windows leading to the street and look out, as if expecting to see Mr. Awtry with a telegraphic dispatch in his hand, and each disappointment she met with on these visits would only add to her intense anxiety. The shades of evening had overshadowed the earth, and Mrs. Wentworth sat at the window of her dwelling waiting the arrival of the news, which would either remove her fears or plunge her in sorrow. Long hours passed, and she had almost despaired of Mr. Awtry's coming that evening, when he walked up the street, and in a few minutes was in the house.

"What news?" gasped Mrs. Wentworth, starting from her seat and meeting him at the door of the apartment.

"Read it, my dear madam. I shall leave that pleasure to you," he replied, handing her a telegraphic dispatch he held in his hand.

Taking the dispatch, Mrs. Wentworth, with trembling fingers, unfolded it and read these words: "Mrs. Eva Wentworth, New Orleans, Louisiana: Yours received. I am safe. Alfred Wentworth." As soon as she had read the dispatch, her pent up anxiety for his safety was allayed, and throwing herself on her knees before a couch, regardless of the presence of Mr. Awtry, who stood looking on, Mrs. Wentworth poured forth a prayer of thanks at the safety of her husband, while tears of joy trickled down her cheeks.

"Allow me to congratulate you, Mrs. Wentworth, on the safety of your husband," said Horace Awtry, after she had become sufficiently composed. "I assure you," he continued, "I feel happy at the knowledge of being the medium through which this welcome intelligence has reached you."

"You have, indeed, proved a friend," she said, extending her hand, which he shook warmly, "and one that I feel I can trust."

"Do not speak of it," he answered; "it is only a natural act of kindness towards one whom I desire to befriend."

"And one I will never cease to forget. Oh! if you had but known how I felt during these past hours of agonizing suspense, you would not have thought lightly of your kind attention; and I am sure when I write Alfred of it, he will not have words sufficient to express his gratitude."

"In my haste to impart the good news to you," said Mr. Awtry, rising, "I almost forgot an engagement I made this evening. It is now getting late, and I must leave. Good evening."

"Good evening," she replied. "I trust you will call to see me soon again."

"With *your* permission I will," he answered, laying particular emphasis on the word "your."

"Certainly," she said. "I shall be most happy to see you at anytime."

"I will call soon, then," he replied. "Good night," and he stepped from the threshold of the house.

"Good night," she said, closing the door.

Horace Awtry stood for a moment near the house; then walking on he muttered: "A politic stroke, that telegraphic dispatch."

CHAPTER FIFTH.

JACKSON, MISSISSIPPI—A HAPPY HOME.

We will now change the scene of our story, and, using the license of all writers, transport the reader to Jackson, the Capital of the great State of Mississippi, and there introduce him or her to other characters who will bear a prominent part in this book.

In the parlor of an elegant resident on Main street, a beautiful girl was sitting with an open book in her hand. She was not, however, reading, as her bright blue eyes rested not on the pages, but were gazing at the half-opened door, as if expecting the arrival of some one. While she is thus musing, we will endeavour to give a description of the fair maiden. Fancy a slight and elegant figure, richly dressed in a robe of *moire antique*, from under the folds of which the daintiest little feet imaginable could be seen. Her features, though not regularly carved, made her, at the name time, very beautiful, while her bright blue eyes and rich golden hair, braided smooth to her forehead, and ornamented with a jewelled tiara, then much worn, lent additional charm to her appearance. Her hands were small, and as Byron, we think, has it, was an undoubted mark of gentle birth.

She remained in this reverie for some time, but was at last aroused by the entrance, unannounced, of a handsome young man dressed in the uniform of a lieutenant, when she started up, and meeting him, said in a half-vexed, half-playful tone:

"Oh, Harry! why did you not come earlier? I have been waiting for your arrival over an hour!"

"Excuse me, dearest," he answered. "I was just on the point of starting from my office when I received a mass of orders from regimental headquarters, which detained me until a few minutes ago. You must, therefore," he continued, "excuse me for this once, and I shall not offend again," and as he spoke he parted the hair from her forehead and pressed a kiss upon her lips.

"I forgive you for this time," she answered, playfully tapping him on the shoulder with her fan; "but the next offence I will not be so likely to excuse."

"I will take good care not to offend again, then," he laughingly said.

The conversation continued for some time in this light way, which lovers will sometimes indulge in, when, assuming a serious countenance, she spoke to him:

"When does your regiment leave for Virginia?"

"I hardly know," he replied, "if it will go to Virginia at all. The Colonel informs me that it is likely the regiment will be sent to Tennessee; so if it is sent there, I will be nearer than you thought."

"What a horrid thing war is!" she said, without appearing to notice his last remarks.

"You are not inclined to show the white feather now, are you?" he said, laughing.

Her bright blue eyes sparkled for a moment, as if repudiating the question; then lowering them she answered: "No, indeed. I would not have a single one that I love remain at home while the Abolitionists are invading our homes."

"Spoken like a brave girl and a true Southern woman," he replied, "and I shall remember your words when I go into battle. It will nerve and inspire me to fight with redoubled courage, when I recollect that I am battling for you." As he spoke he gazed at her with mingled pride and affection, and for some minutes they remained gazing at each other with that affection which springs from

"Two souls with but a single thought— Two hearts that beat as one."

Oh, Love! ye goddess of all that is blissful and elevating in man! How thy devotees bow down to thy shrine and offer all that they possess to purchase but a smile from thee! And when you have cast your favors on some happy mortal, and the pure feeling of affection becomes centered on woman, the fairest flower from Eden, how should not mankind cherish the gift you have bestowed upon him, and look upon it as the first and priceless object on earth, and but second to one above in heaven!

The lovers remained in this silence, which spoke more than words could have done, until the entrance of a tall and venerable looking gentleman of about fifty years of age. As soon as he entered, they rose up together, the young lady addressing him as "father," and the young man as "doctor."

"How are you, Harry, my boy? give me a kiss, Em'," he said, in one breath, as he shook the young man warmly by the hand and pressed a parental kiss on the brow of his daughter. "Pretty warm weather, this," he continued, speaking to the young man; "it is almost stifling."

"Suppose we step out on the balcony, pa," said the young lady; "it is much cooler there."

"Ha, ha, ha," he laughed; "you had not found that out until I entered. However," he went on, "do you both go out there. I am certain you will do better without than with me."

His daughter blushed, but made no reply, and the young man removing two chairs to the balcony, they both left the old gentleman, who, turning up the gas, proceeded to read his evening *Mississippian*.

Dr. James Humphries was one of the oldest and most respectable citizens of Jackson, and was looked upon with great esteem by all who knew him. He had been a medical practitioner in that city from the time it was nothing more than a little village, until railroad connections had raised it to be a place of some consequence, and the capital of the State. He had married when a young man, but of all his children, none remained but his daughter Emma, in gaining whom he lost a much-loved wife, she having died in child-birth.

At the time we write, Emma Humphries was betrothed to Henry Shackleford, a young lawyer of fine ability, but who was, like many of his countrymen, a soldier in the service of his country, and been elected first lieutenant of the "Mississippi Rifles."

We will now leave them for the present, and in the next chapter introduce the reader to two other characters.

CHAPTER SIXTH

THE SPECTATOR AND EXTORTIONER.

Mr. Jacob Swartz was sitting in the back room of his store on Main street counting a heap of gold and silver coins which lay on a table before him. He was a small, thin-bodied man, with little gray eyes, light hair and aquiline nose. He was of that nationality generally known in this country as "Dutch;" but having been there for over twenty years, he had become naturalized, and was now a citizen of the chivalrous States of Mississippi, a fact of which he prided himself considerably.

Mr. Swartz was busily engaged counting his money, when a little boy, who seemed, from a similarity of features, to be his son appeared at the door, and mentioned that Mr. Elder desired to see him.

"Vot can he vant?" said Mr. Swartz. Then as if recollecting, he continued: "I suppose it is apout that little shtore he vants to rent me. Tell him to come in."

The boy withdrew, and a few seconds after a tall and scrupulously dressed gentleman, with his coat buttoned up to the throat, and wearing a broad rimmed hat, entered the room. This was Mr. James Elder, a citizen of Jackson, but not a native of the State. He came from Kentucky several years before, and was a man with "Southern principles." To do him justice, we will say that he was really true friend to the South, which fact may have been not only from principle, but from his being a large slaveholder. He was also the possessor of a considerable amount of landed property and real estate, among which were several buildings in Jackson.. He was also looked upon by the *world*, as very charitable man, being always busy collecting money from the people in aid of some benevolent object, and occasionally his name would appear in the newspapers, accompanied by a flattering compliment to his generosity, as the donor of a liberal amount of money to some charitable institution or society. There were people, however, who said that the poor families, who hired a series of tenement buildings he possessed in the lower part of the city, were very often hard pressed for their rent, and more than once turned out for non-payment. These reports were considered as slanders, for being a member, and one of the pillars of the Methodist Church, no one, for a moment, believed that he would be guilty of so unfeeling an action.

On entering the room, Mr. James Elder made a stiff bow to Mr. Swartz, and declining the hand offered to him, as if it were contamination to touch the person of one of God's likeness, dusted a chair and sat down opposite his host.

"Vell, Mr. Elder, have you decided whether I can get the shtore or not? Tis place of mine is in very pad orter, and I tinks yours vill shust suit me," began Mr. Swartz, after a silence of about three minutes.

"Yes, Mr. Swartz, I think you can have the place, if you and I can come to terms about the price of the rent, which must be payable always in advance," replied Mr. Elder.

"I tont care," answered Mr. Swartz. "I would as soon pay you in advance as not. But vot price to you charge?"

"I charge fifty dollars per month," was the short answer.

"Vell, dat vill do; and I suppose you vill give me the shtore for von year certain?"

"I am not decided about that," replied Mr. Elder, "as I do not like to bind myself for any given time; for," he continued, "there is no telling what may be the worth of a store in six months."

"I vould not take it unless I could get a lease by the year," replied Mr. Swartz; "for the fact is, I have made a large contract with the government, and vill have to extend by pisness."

Mr. Elder remained thoughtful for a few moments; then he replied: "As you wont take it unless I give a lease for twelve months, I will do so on one condition: that on your failure to pay the rent monthly in advance, you forfeit the lease, and I am at liberty to demand your removal without any notice."

"Shust as you like," he replied, "for I know te monish vill always pe ready in advance."

"Well, I shall have the lease drawn out to-day and bring it to you to sign," said Mr. Elder, rising and putting on his gloves. "Good morning; be here at three o'clock, as I shall call round at that hour," and with those words he left the room, and the Dutchman resumed the counting of his money.

CHAPTER SEVENTH.

THE HUSBAND A PRISONER—EXILE OF THE SOLDIER'S WIFE.

Months rolled on, during which time Mrs. Wentworth was cheered by many kind and affectionate letters from her husband, who had not been sick a day since his departure from home. One of the letters received from him stated that he had been detailed from his regiment to act as clerk in Brigadier General Floyd's adjutant general's office, his superior intelligence fitting him admirably for such an office; and the next letter from him was dated at Fort Donelson, whence General Floyd had been ordered with his brigade.

Fort Donelson fell. We need not record here the heroic defense and stubborn fighting of the Confederate forces, and their unfortunate capture afterwards. These are matters of history, and should be recorded by the historian, and not the novelist. Sufficient to say, that in the last day's fight Alfred Wentworth, having received a severe wound in the arm, was marching to the rear, when an officer, dressed in the garb of a lieutenant, who was lying on the field, called faintly to him, and on his going up, he observed that the lieutenant's left leg was fearfully mangled by a fragment of shell, and was bleeding so profusely, that, unless medical aid was quickly procured, he would die. Forgetting his own wound, which was very painful, he lifted the officer on his shoulder and bore him to the hospital, where his leg was immediately attended to, and his life saved. The severity of his own wound, and the length of time which elapsed before any attention was paid to it, brought on a severe fever, and on the escape of General Floyd, he was delirious and unable to accompany him. He was, therefore, sent to Chicago, and placed in the same hospital with the lieutenant whose life he had saved.

On their recovery, which was about the same time, Lieutenant Shackleford—for it was he—and Alfred Wentworth were both sent to "Camp Douglas," the military prison near Chicago.

On the receipt of the news in New Orleans, that Fort Donelson and nearly its entire garrison had surrendered, Mrs. Wentworth underwent another long suspense of excitement and anxiety, which was, however, partially allayed by the intelligence that General Floyd and staff had escaped. But as the weeks rolled on, and she received no letter from her husband, the old fear that he may have been killed came over her again, until relieved by seeing his name as being among the wounded at the Chicago hospital in one of the city papers.

In mentioning these hours of grief and suspense on the part of Mrs. Wentworth, it must not be understood that we are representing a weak-minded and cowardly woman. On the contrary, Mrs. Wentworth would have rather heard that her husband was killed than one word spoken derogatory to his courage, and would never have consented to his remaining at home, while so many of his countrymen were hurrying to protect their country from invasion. Her suspense and grief at the intelligence of a battle in which her husband was engaged, were only the natural feeling of an affectionate wife. At that moment she was no longer the patriot daughter of the South; she was the wife and mother, and none should blame her for her anxiety to know the fate of one so much loved as her husband, and the father of her children.

Soon after her husband was taken prisoner, Mrs. Wentworth observed that Horace Awtry became more assiduous in his attentions to her. Every day he would call with presents for her children, and several times small packages of bank-bills were found in the parlor, which, when presented to him, he would always disclaim being the owner of; and although Mrs. Wentworth truly believed that they had been left there by him, the kind and respectful tone he used to her, and the intense interest he appeared to take in the welfare of her children, were such that she never imagined, for a moment, he was using this means to cloak a vile and unmanly purpose. Once, and only once, was she made aware that the scandal tongues of her neighbors were being used detrimental to her honor; and then the information was given by her slave Elsy, who overheard a conversation between two of her neighbors not at all complimentary to her, and which the faithful negress lost no time in repeating to her mistress, with the very indignant remark that, "ef dem people nex' doh fancy dey can do anyting to take away your name, dey's much mistaken, as I will tell you ebery ting dey say 'bout you, an' you will know what to do." Mrs. Wentworth made no reply to the negro, but on the next visit of Mr. Awtry's, she candidly told him what had been said of her in consequence of his visits. He appeared very much surprised, but told her that such scandalous remarks, emanating as they did out of pure malice, should not be noticed, as all who were acquainted with her knew very well that her character and fair name were above suspicion. With that the subject was dropped, and he continued paying her his visits.

New Orleans fell into the hands of the enemy, and the whole Confederacy was convulsed, as if shaken by an earthquake. None anticipated such a thing, and its fall brought misery to thousands. The enemy had scarcely taken possession, than Horace Awtry and his bosom friend, Charles Bell, went to the provost marshal's office and took the oath of allegiance, after proving, entirely to the satisfaction of the Yankees, that they were Northern, and had always been Union men. Mr. Awtry immediately received a commission in the Federal army, and by his willingness to point out prominent "secession" men and women, soon ingratiated himself in the favor of "Beast Butler."

No sooner had he gained the favor of Butler, than his attentions to Mrs. Wentworth changed to that of unmanly presumption, and at last he had the baseness to make proposals at once dishonorable to her as a lady of virtue and position in society, and disgraceful to him as a man. These propositions were accompanied by a threat to have her turned out of the house and exiled from New Orleans. With a spirit worthy of a Southern woman, she indignantly spurned his base offers and ordered him never to place his feet across the threshold of her house, at the same time defying to do his worse. He left her, declaring that she should be turned out of the city, and a few days after, in proof of his threat, an order was presented to her, signed by General Butler, commanding her to leave the city.

Her faithful slave, Elsy, shed bitter tears on hearing that her kind mistress would have to leave New Orleans, and declared that she would not remain in the city, but would follow her.

"But they will not let you go with me, Elsy," said Mrs. Wentworth. "You are free now, they say, to do as you like—you are no longer belonging to me."

"I ain't a gwine to stay here, missis," replied the negro, "for any money in dis world, and if dey wont let me go out wid you, I will come arter you by myself."

"Well, Elsy," said Mrs. Wentworth, "I do not force you to leave New Orleans, but should you get out, come to me at Jackson. You are a good girl, and I shall not forget your fidelity."

"I'll be dere, shure," said the negro, quite pleased at the permission to follow her mistress if she could.

Mrs. Wentworth immediately set to work packing up a few necessaries, and with the small amount of money she had left awaited the next morning, when she would start for Pass Manchac.

On the following morning she proceeded to the boat, amid the cries and lamentations of the faithful Elsy, and with throbbing heart and many sighs gazed on her loved city until it had receded from her view.

On arriving at the "Pass" she was about to step from the boat, when a hand was laid upon her shoulder, and looking round she observed Mr. Awtry, dressed in the full uniform of a Yankee captain, standing by her.

"Are you determined to leave home," he said, "and all its pleasures; and starve in the rebel lines? Why not accept my offer and lead a life of ease and affluence. Your husband shall never know of our connection, and thus you will be spared many a weary day and night working for bread to feed your children."

She looked at him for a moment with all that withering scorn and indignation which outraged virtue and innocence can assume, and then said: "Leave me! Go to the land from whence you came and make such offers to the women there, but remember now you are speaking to a Southern woman."

"But think a moment, and—" he began.

"Leave me this instant," she said excitedly, "or I shall call others with more the heart of men than you to my assistance. Accept your offer?" she continued with all the scorn she could use. "Accept such an offer from a *Yankee*! Go, I would despise and hate were you not too despicable for either feeling of enmity."

Several persons approaching at that moment, he moved away hurriedly after hissing in her ear: "Take your choice. In either one way or the other I am revenged on you for the way you rejected my addresses in past years."

She landed on the shore, and a few minutes after the boat moved back on its way to New Orleans, when taking her small trunk in her hands the soldier's wife, with her two children, started on their long and lively march. For where? She knew not. There she was, an utter stranger with two tender children, far from her home, and with only two hundred dollars in money. Where could she go to for support. Her husband was in a foreign prison, and she a wanderer in a strange State. Her heart sank within her, and the soldier's wife wept. Aye, wept! Not tears of regret at what she had sacrificed, but tears of loneliness. Who would not weep if they were parted from those they love, and were cast in a strange land without a friend, and with scarcely any means?

We leave the soldier's wife for a brief while, and transport the reader to her husband. Her trials have commenced—God help her!

CHAPTER EIGHTH.

THE PRISONERS—THE HUSBAND AND THE LOVER.

We stated that on the recovery of Alfred Wentworth and Lieutenant Shackleford from their wounds, both were sent to Camp Douglas together, and as Alfred had no regiment of his own captured, the lieutenant promptly requested him to become one of his mess. The generous courage exhibited by Alfred Wentworth, and the fact that but for his chivalric attention, he should have died on the bloody field of Fort Donelson, had created a feeling of gratitude in Lieutenant Shackleford for his preserver, which, on closer acquaintance, had ripened into a warm friendship, and he soon made Alfred acquainted with the fact of his betrothal to Emma Humphries, and Alfred in turn would speak of his wife and children in such tones of affection as only those who love can use. They would sit down for hours and converse on the loved ones at home, thus wiling away the sad and lonely hours of a prison life, until the news was received in Chicago of the fall of New Orleans. Although he bitterly regretted his native city having fallen into the hands of the enemy, the opportunity which it presented of once more being able to correspond with his wife, made him feel happier, and as soon as mail communication was received with the city, he requested and obtained permission to write her.

Alfred Wentworth had not the slightest idea that Horace Awtry would ever dare to offend his wife, much less to offer infamous proposals, and on their being refused have her driven from the home he had placed her in. It is true that his wife had written to him that Mr. Awtry had renewed his acquaintance with her, but her statements of his kind attention to her and the children, and her mentioning the eager manner in which he had relieved her anxiety after the battle of the 21st of July, 1861, instead of raising any suspicion on his part of the honesty and purity of his motives, only made him return thanks in his heart for the previous kindness shown to his wife.

On obtaining permission to write her, he immediately penned a long and affectionate letter which was forwarded. For many days after he remained in a long suspense for the expected answer, as he never believed for a moment that she would delay answering him, but as days rolled into weeks, and no letter came, while the other prisoners from New Orleans received letters regularly, he became alarmed, and spoke his fears to Shackleford.

"Do not be afraid of any harm having occurred to her, Alf," said the lieutenant, after listening attentively to his friend's words. "You may depend that your letter never reached her, and she, in ignorance whether you escaped unhurt from the engagement, cannot write, not knowing where you are."

"It is not her silence which troubles me as much as the knowledge that she possess no other money than Confederate notes," replied Alfred. "How she will manage to support herself and the children God only knows."

"Have you not friends there?" enquired Harry.

"Yes, but I cannot depend on them for assistance, for two reasons: first, because from the disordered state of the money market in New Orleans, they are almost as badly off as she is; and second, I am quite certain that Eva would rather starve than ask for charity."

"Charity!", echoed his companion. "Do you call it charity to assist another situated as your wife is, particularly where her husband is far from her fighting for his country?"

"You do not know the people of New Orleans," replied Alfred. "No matter how kindly a favor may be bestowed on them, it is still considered charity, and though dire necessity may induce them to accept aid if proffered, the knowledge that they were eating the bread of charity, would embitter each mouthful."

"Pooh, pooh," said his friend, "all these fine notions would do very well before the war, but at the present time the least we think of them the better."

"It is all very well for you to speak that way," answered Alfred, "for you have no wife and children to cause uneasiness, but I cannot be otherwise than anxious to know what has become of her, that I receive no letters, while other prisoners have had theirs regularly by mail."

"An unfortunate fact, which you may depend has been caused by no other reason than the neglect of the Yankee officers to forward your letters," said Harry, then continuing: "Come, cheer up, and throw aside your dullness. Another battle like that of Shiloh, will give the South as many Yankee prisoners as they have of us, and then ho! for home and the "Sunny South!" As soon as we return, I will take you to Jackson, and then you can write your wife to come out, and she can live with my mother, if you are not too proud to accept my hospitality."

"Thank you," he replied, "but I must first wait until we are exchanged, and God knows when that will be."

"Why, man, I tell you there is no doubt of our whipping the Yanks and capturing a lot of them in the next battle; then adieu to Camp Douglas, and hurrah for the Confederacy once more!" replied Harry, taking his companion by the arm, and dragging him to their tent where dinner had been placed in readiness for them.

CHAPTER NINTH.

ROOM TO RENT.

We must now return to my heroine, who, with her two children, we left slowly travelling toward Jackson, Mississippi. On arriving at Ponchatula, she took the cars on the New Orleans, Jackson and Great Northern Railroad, and in a few hours was in Jackson. On arriving there she proceeded to the Bowman House, and purchasing a newspaper eagerly scanned the columns to find an advertisement of rooms to rent, knowing full well that, with her limited means, she would never be able to remain at the hotel, or live at a boarding house.

After looking for some time, without finding the desired advertisement, her eye at last lit upon the following notice under the heading of "To rent:"

"TO RENT,

"Unfurnished rooms in the one-story tenement buildings on —— street. For particulars, apply to the undersigned at his office on Main street, near the State House.

Jamie Elder."

After reading it she folded the paper, and remained musing for several minutes, when rising up she went to her children, and, kissing them, told them she was going out for a few minutes, and to play like good children until her return. She then left the hotel, and, after some little trouble, at last found out the office of Mr. Elder, which she entered.

"Is Mr. Elder in?" she inquired of a clerk.

"Yes, madam," he replied.

"Can I see him?" she asked.

He gave her no answer, but going to an adjoining door, half opened it, and announced, in a loud voice, that a lady desired to see Mr. Elder.

"Admit her," was the reply of that gentleman.

Mrs. Wentworth passed the desk, and, entering the room from whence the voice proceeded, found herself in the presence of Mr. Elder, who was seated in an arm chair reading a newspaper.

"Be seated, madam," he said, rising and handing her a chair. "What can I have the honor of doing for you this morning?"

"This is your advertisement, I believe," she replied, handing him the newspaper.

"Yes, madam," he answered, looking at her through his spectacles.

"Well, sir, it is my desire to rent one of the rooms."

"You, madam!" he replied, evidently surprised at her question.

"Yes, sir," she replied; "I am a refugee from New Orleans, having been driven from there by General Butler. My husband is now a prisoner of war in the hands of the enemy, and my means being limited, I am compelled to live economically."

"Ahem, ahem," said Mr. Elder, clearing his throat; "indeed, madam, I sympathise with you. This war has cast many people homeless and in need throughout the country. I sympathize with you, *indeed* I do," and he looked on her in the most benevolent manner possible.

"Well, sir, what is the price charged for the rent of one of your rooms?" asked Mrs. Wentworth after a few moments' silence.

"Well, ah—well, ah—you see, my dear madam, the price of everything has gone up immensely," he replied.

"And what do you charge for the room?" she asked.

"Well, ah, I think sixteen dollars per month as cheap as I could possible rent it," he answered finally.

"I will take it, then, by the month," she answered, rising, "and will go into possession to-day."

"Well, ah, my dear madam, it is a rule I have always made, only to rent my houses for the money, paid in advance—not that I have the *least* apprehension of your inability to pay me, but you see it never does any good to deviate from fixed rules."

"I am perfectly filling to pay you in advance," she replied, taking her port-moniæ from her pocket and handing him the advance pay for one month's rent.

Calling a clerk, Mr. Elder handed him the money, and ordered a receipt to be made out; then turning to Mrs. Wentworth, he said:

"There is another thing, I desire to have you understand, madam, and agree to. The fall of New Orleans has occasioned the inflation of all kinds of real estate in price, and this, added to the rapid manner in which Confederate notes are depreciating in value, may compel me to raise the price of rent. I would, therefore, like you to agree, that in no way am I bound for any time longer than the month you have paid for, to take the present price; and another thing I desire is, that you agree not to take advantage of the stay law, in the event of non-payment, or refusal to pay any additional price I may charge. In making these conditions, madam," he continued, "I must not be understood to say that the contingencies mentioned are at all likely to occur, as I trust and hope they will not; but at the same time, I only desire to avoid all deviation from my usual course of doing business."

"Any terms you may desire I will agree to," she replied in an absent manner, "as I wish to remove from the hotel, the charges there being above my means."

"Very well, madam, very well," he responded.

After the clerk had brought the receipt for the months rent, Mr. Elder rose from his chair, and, requesting Mrs. Wentworth to remain seated for a few minutes, left the apartment. He shortly after returned with a printed document in his hand, which he requested her to sign. Without reading the paper, she obeyed his request, and, receiving the key of the room she had just rented, requested that Mr. Elder would have her shown where it was situated. Calling a negro boy, who was lounging at the door, he directed him to accompany Mrs. Wentworth to ---- street and show her the rooms. With that he made a low bow, and she left following the boy.

"Humph!" said Mr. Elder, half aloud, as soon as she had left. "I do not care much about hiring my rooms to such tenants. Refugees are certainly becoming as thick as locusts in the State, and are nearly all as poor as Job. However, I have made myself secure against any excuse for pay on the ground of poverty, by the paper she signed," and with these reflections, that worthy gentleman re-entered his room, and was soon deeply interested in his newspaper.

CHAPTER TENTH.

THE NEW HOME.

Mrs. Wentworth followed the boy till he arrived in front of series of wretched looking rooms, situated on one of the miserable lanes with which Jackson abounds. Stopping in front of one of them, he pointed to it, and with no other words than "Dem is de room, ma'm," walked off. Taking the key, which Mr. Elder had previously given her, she opened the door and entered.

Mrs. Wentworth's heart sank within her as she viewed the wretched looking apartment. The interior of the room was exceedingly dirty, while the faded paper, which once gaudily adorned it, now hung in shreds from the walls. The fireplace was broken up, and disgusting words were written in every part of the room. It had been, in fact, the lodging of a woman of dissolute character, who had been accustomed to gather a crowd of debauched characters in her apartment nightly, but who, from a failure to pay her rent, had been turned out by Mr. Elder. The other apartments were still occupied by abandoned women; but of this fact Mrs. Wentworth was not aware.

As she looked at the room a feeling of indescribable sadness crept over her, and a sigh of bitterness burst from her throbbing bosom. It was, however, not to be helped; she had already paid the rent, and was compelled to keep it for the month. Sadly she left the room, and locking it after her, repaired to a store to purchase a few necessary articles of furniture.

On entering a store, the first person she saw was Mr. Swartz, who had, by this time, risen from the lowly position of a grocer to that of a "General wholesale and retail merchant," as the sign over his door very pompously announced.

Mr. Swartz remained on his seat at her entrance, barely raising his eyes to sec who had entered. She stood for a few moments, when, seeing that no one appeared to notice her presence, she walked up to him and informed him that she wished to purchase a few pieces of furniture.

"Vot kind do you vant?" he inquired, without moving from his seat.

"A small bedstead, three or four chairs, a table and a washstand," she answered.

"Look at them and see vich you like te best," he said, "and I vill tell you te brice."

After a little search, Mrs. Wentworth selected the plainest and most homely she could find of all the articles she desired, and, turning to him, inquired what the price would be.

"Te pedstead is forty tollars; te chairs is three tollars apiece; te taple is twenty tollars; and to washstand is fourteen," he replied.

"And how much will that amount to, altogether?" she asked.

"Eighty-six tollars," he responded.

"Can you take no less, sir?" she asked.

"No, ma'am," he answered. "I have put one brice, and if you don't vant to pay it you can leave it."

Taking out the desired amount, she paid him without making any further remark, and requested that they would be sent after her. Calling a drayman, Mr. Swartz told him to follow her with the furniture, and he returned to his seat, satisfied with having made sixty dollars on the eighty-six, received from Mrs. Wentworth, the furniture having been bought at sheriff's sale for a mere trifle.

Having purchased a few other household utensils, Mrs. Wentworth proceeded to the Bowman House, from which, after paying her bill, she removed her children, and, followed by the dray with her furniture, proceeded to the wretched hovel site had rented. Her stock of money had now been reduced to less than sixty dollars, and with this she embarked upon the world with two tender children.

After paying the drayman, who was a kind-hearted negro, and getting him to erect the bedstead, he departed, and a feeling of desolation and loneliness spread its dark shadows over the heart of Mrs. Wentworth. Seating herself on a chair, with her two children clinging to her knees, the long pent up fountain of grief burst forth, and tears bedewed the cheeks of the Soldier's Wife; tears, such as only those who have felt the change of fortune, can shed; tears, which, like the last despairing cry of the desolate, can only be answered in heaven!

CHAPTER ELEVENTH.

THE ATTEMPTED ESCAPE.

We must now return to Alfred, whom we left in a disconsolate mood at Camp Douglas, with his friend trying to cheer his spirits. But he could think of nothing else but his absent wife, until at last he determined to attempt an escape. The idea once in his mind could not be dismissed. He, therefore, informed Harry of his intention, and asked if he thought it feasible, or likely to result in success.

"So far as the feasibility of the attempt is concerned," observed Harry, as soon as Alfred had concluded, "I think it could be attempted. But about the result, you will have to trust to luck."

"I am aware of that," he replied. "But I do not know how the attempt can possibly be made. The camp is so well guarded, that an attempt to escape is almost hopeless of success."

"Pshaw! If you are determined to go, I see nothing to prevent your making the attempt. If it even fails, the most that will be done to you by the Federals is closer confinement."

"I do not care much about that risk," he replied. "My desire is to form some plan of escape. Can you devise one by which I can get away?"

"That is a difficult task," said Harry. "But as we are of the same desire, I suppose something must be done. What do you say about digging a tunnel, and escaping by that route?"

"That is a very good idea; but it will take too long," replied Alfred. "Besides which, what are we to do with the dirt that is dug up?"

"I never thought of that," he answered. "But now that you have reminded me of it, I do not believe the plan will suit. Some other must be devised, but what it is to be, I cannot, for the life of me, imagine."

"What do you say to scaling the walls?" asked Alfred.

"A very good idea it would be, if we had anything to scale them with," he replied.

"Suppose we tear up our blankets and make a rope of them."

"How will you attach the rope to the wall?" asked Harry.

"We can easily get a hook of wire and throw it over. It will be certain to catch," he replied.

"Very likely," observed Harry, drily, "and make such confounded noise, that the first thing we heard after, it would be a Minie ball whistling past our ears; or should it catch without making any noise, the chances are that, when one of us ascends, it will be to meet the burly form of some Dutch sentinel traversing the walk. The idea is not feasible; so we must think of something else."

"I do not know what to think," replied Alfred; "and the probability is, that if I even did, you would find some objection to its performance."

"That is true," answered Harry, laughing, "and I accept the reproach in the spirit it is given. It will never do for us to be raising objections to every plan offered, for that will not hasten our escape."

"Then think of something else, and I will acquiesce, no matter how extravagant it may be," said Alfred. "I am tired of this cursed prison, and intend to get away by some means or other."

"It is all very good to talk about getting away," said Harry. "For the matter of that, I am as anxious to leave as you are, but in the name of wonder, how are we going to manage it?"

"That is the very thing I desire to consult you about. We certainly will never escape, unless we make the attempt; but in what manner we are to attempt it, is exactly what I desire to know."

"What do you say to bribing one of the sentinels?" asked Harry.

"Where will we get the means from?" inquired Alfred. "I have some Confederate Treasury notes, but they will not be any temptation to a Yankee."

"Leave me to find the means," replied Harry. "I have a fine gold watch, and about seventy dollars in gold. These will be sufficient, I think, to attempt the cupidity of any Dutchman in the Yankee army."

"And how do you propose offering the bribe?" Alfred inquired.

"I shall look out for the first chance to speak to the sentinel at the gate, some time during the day, and will make the necessary preparations to escape to-night, if the Yankee will accept my offer."

"That will do very well," observed Alfred, "There is one thing, however, I must remind you of. It will not do to offer the sentinel all your gold, for we will require money to pay our way into Tennessee."

"Do you never fear that," replied Harry. "I will be certain to reserve enough funds for our expenses. It does not cost much at any time to travel through these Northern States."

"Well, I trust to you to make all the necessary arrangements," replied Alfred. "I am determined not to remain in this place, with my mind so disturbed about my wife and children. If I can only reach the Confederate lines safely, I will have no difficulty in hearing from New Orleans."

"I will make every effort to facilitate an escape," remarked Harry; "and if my penetrating qualities do not deceive me, there is a sentinel at the gate to-day, who would not be averse to taking a bribe, even if it permits a "rebel" to escape. Cheer up, my friend," he continued. "I will guarantee that your wife and children are all well and happy, except a natural anxiety on your account."

Alfred made no reply, and the two friends shortly after separated.

Harry kept an assiduous watch for an opportunity to speak with the sentinel. The time for the man to remain on guard expired, however, without any favorable chance presenting itself. He was, therefore, compelled to wait until the evening, when the same sentinel would be again on guard, before he could attempt to bribe him. At four o'clock he was posted, and after some hesitation, Harry determined to address him. Walking up as soon as he perceived no one near the man, he called out to him.

"Vot to deuce do you vant? you rebel," asked the sentinel in a broad Dutch accent.

"Will you let me come a little nearer?" Harry inquired, perceiving that the distance between the guard and himself too great for a conversation.

"Vot do you vant to come a leetle nearer for?" asked the sentinel.

"I want to talk to you," he replied, making a motion of his hand to indicate that he wished to converse in secret.

The sentinel, looking carefully around to be certain that no one was near at hand who could perceive him, beckoned to Harry to approach. The young man went forward cautiously, as the numerous sentinels around the wall were likely to perceive him, and would not hesitate to fire if they imagined he was about to attempt an escape. As soon as he reached the sentinel, he made known his wishes, and ended by offering the man his watch and forty dollars in gold if he would permit himself and his friend to pass the gate at night. At the same time he promised the man he would take all the responsibility in the event of detection or re-capture.

The sentinel listened attentively, and at first appeared unwilling to receive the bribe, but upon Harry representing to him that there was no chance of his agency in the escape being discovered, he finally consented to receive it. It was, therefore, arranged between them, that at twelve o'clock that night the two prisoners should start. The signal was to be a faint whistle, which would ultimate to the guard that they were there, if it was answered they should advance, but if not they should return, as his silence would either indicate that he was not alone, or that he was not on his post. Everything having been amicably arranged between them, Harry promised to pay the bribe as soon as they had reached the gate. This the fellow demurred to at first, but as Harry was determined, not to pay over the watch and forty dollars, until the hour of their departure, he was compelled to assent.

On Harry's return to his tent, he found Alfred reading a Yankee pictorial newspaper.

"Well," he remarked, looking up from his paper as soon as Harry entered.

"Everything progresses finely," replied Harry.

"Have you been able to speak to the sentinel?" he asked.

"I have seen him, and made all the necessary arrangements," Harry replied.

"And when will we leave," Alfred asked.

"To-night at twelve is the time fixed between us," he replied. "The fellow appeared unwilling at first, but a little persuasion with a sight at the watch and money, was too much for his nature, and he yielded to my wishes."

"Then everything goes on well, if the fellow does not play us false," Alfred remarked.

"That is a risk we are bound to run," replied Harry. "I think the fellow means to be honest, if a man can be honest who agrees to allow a prisoner to escape, who is placed under his charge."

"Did you inform him there were two of us who desired to leave," asked Alfred.

"Yes," was the reply; "I would never have bothered to escape and run the risk of re-capture and harsh treatment, did not you desire to leave this place, and the trip could as well be made with you as otherwise."

Alfred pressed his friend's hand warmly, as he replied. "Thank you, Harry, I trust I will be able to return the kindness you have shown me, at some future and more favorable time."

"Poh, poh!" he replied. "Don't speak of it. The kindness has been paid for long ago," pointing to his wound as he spoke.

"I expect we may as well make preparations to leave," remarked Alfred, after a moment's pause.

"Preparations!" echoed his friend, "What in the name of all that is glorious, do you require any preparations for?" and then, he added dryly, "there is one thing certain, my trunk (?) is already packed, although I don't know if yours is."

"A truce to joking about trunks," replied Alfred, "but seriously you must be aware that we cannot leave here without being dressed in citizens clothes."

"The thunder!" exclaimed Harry, "are you going to raise any more objections?"

"No," he replied, "but it is absolutely necessary that we shall be apparelled in different clothes to those of a soldier."

"I think we can get a couple of suits to borrow from the officers, but how I will get them, without their knowing our intention to escape, is a matter of much difficulty. If they should once know it, the whole crowd will desire to leave with us."

"That would be unreasonable on their part," replied Alfred. "They must be aware that every man cannot get away at the same time, and to desire or attempt such a thing would be to ensure the re-capture of every man."

"Well, I will start now on the borrowing expedition, and by some subterfuge, be saved the necessity of informing any person of our intention."

Having moved off as he spoke, and proceeding to the tent of a brother officer, succeeded in borrowing a citizens' coat and pants without exciting any suspicion of his intended escape. At the next place he went to, a few remarks were made, but upon his informing the Captain to whom he applied, that he desired to have his uniform renovated, and had no change of clothing while that was being done. The citizens' clothes were cordially loaned, and he returned to Alfred with a joyous heart.

"What luck have you had?" enquired Alfred as soon as he returned.

"See for yourself," was the reply of Harry, as he threw down the coats and pants.

"Then everything needed is procured," he observed.

"Yes," replied Harry. "We must now mix with the other prisoners, as if nothing was transpiring in our minds, like an attempt to escape. It will be no use keeping away from them, as it is likely to excite suspicion."

The two friends left the tent and proceeded to where a group of prisoners were seated. Their appearance was greeted with cheers, as Harry was a universal favorite among both officers and men, on account of his lively and genial temper, combined with a fine voice for music—an accomplishment that with soldiers endears, and makes a favorite of any person possessing it.

He was soon called upon for a song, and in accordance with the request commenced a song, and soon the rich and clear voice of the young man rang out on the air of the soft twilight. He sang of home, and as each word fell with distinctness on the ears of the soldiers, who grouped around him, each heart throbbed with emotion, and each mind wandered back to the distant land, where, in the mansion, or in the little cottage, loved ones there dwelt, pining for those who were now prisoners in a foreign country.

The hour of nine having arrived, the soldiers dispersed to their respective quarters, and soon after the command "lights out" was uttered in stentorian notes. Long and anxiously the two friends remained lying on their bunks in the tent, awaiting the hour of twelve. Each moment seemed an hour to Alfred Wentworth, whose mind was wrought up to a pitch of excitement, almost unendurable. Several times he rose from his bed and paced the tent. At last the long wished for hour arrived. Harry who had been smoking all the night, looked at his watch by the faint light the fire of his segar emitted, and perceived that it was only five minutes for twelve. Crossing over to the bunk on which Alfred was lying, he whispered: "It is time." Silently they put on the citizens clothes borrowed in the evening, and left the tent. The night had changed from the pleasant, starry evening to a black and dismal gloom. Heavy clouds covered the skies, giving every indication of rain. The night was just such a one for an escape, and although the darkness was so intense, that it was impossible for the eye to penetrate a distance of five paces, both felt that their chance of escape was accelerated.

"Give me your hand," whispered Harry, as soon as they had left the tent.

"Do you know the direct way to the gate," asked Alfred,

"Yes," he replied, "cease speaking now and follow me. The least whisper may be heard, and then our attempt will be foiled."

Grasping the hand of his friend, Alfred followed him, and they moved with noiseless tread toward the gate. As soon as he descried the faint light of the sentinel's lamp near him, Harry stopped, and stooping down gave a faint whistle. For some time no answer was returned. The two friends remained in almost breathless suspense awaiting the signal. At last it was returned, and moving forward, they reached the gate.

"Here," whispered Harry to the sentinel, as he handed him the watch and money.

The man raised the little lantern near him, and looked at the bribe to see that it was all right. "Pass on," he said.

As Harry and his friend passed the gate, the former perceived several forms flit across the darkness, and a suspicion of treachery instantly flashed through his mind.

"We are betrayed," he whispered to Alfred.

"No matter, let us push boldly forward," was the reply.

They had not moved ten paces before the command "Halt" given.

"Push on!" exclaimed Alfred, darting forward.

The two friends moved on at a rapid run, when a volley of musketry was fired at them. Harry escaped unhurt and continued running at the top of his speed, and not until he had gone a considerable distance, did he discover that his friend was not with him. It was, however, too late for him to turn back, and entering Chicago, he made his way through the city, and continued his journey.

At the fire of the Federals, Alfred received four wounds; and sunk without a word to the ground. The enemy shortly after coming up found him insensible, and conveyed his inanimate body to the hospital. He was dangerously wounded, and the physicians declared there was but little hope of his recovery.

Two weeks after this unfortunate occurrence, a cartel for the exchange of prisoners was agreed upon between the Federal and Confederate authorities, and the prisoners at Camp Douglas were transported to Vicksburg. The doctors declared that Alfred was not in a state to be removed, and was left at the hospital. His condition at that time was very precarious. One of the balls that had entered his body could not be found, and the wound was kept open with the view to discovering where it had lodged. His agony of mind at the failure of his attempt to escape had retarded his recovery in a great degree, and when the information came that the prisoners were about to be exchanged, and he was declared unable to be removed, it added further to his detriment. A fever seized him, and for many days he remained on his bed, hovering between life and death.

CHAPTER TWELFTH.

THE STARVING CHILDREN.

Long weeks rolled on, and the small sum possessed by Mrs. Wentworth, had been entirely exhausted. She had, however, by sewing, contrived to supply herself and children with food. It was the same old tale of sleepless nights of toil. Often the grey streak which heralds the morning, would find her still pouring over her work, while her two children were sleeping on the bed in one corner of the room. At times she would cease her work, and think for long hours on the loved husband, now a prisoner in the hands of the Federals. In those hours, tears would course her cheeks, as the stern reality of her position presented itself; to know that he was absent, while she was leading a life of penury and toil. Still she struggled on. When at times despair rose up before her like a demon, and she felt herself about to succumb to it, the memory of her absent husband, and the sight of her loved children, would nerve the soldier's wife to bear with fortitude the misery to which she had been reduced.

And thus she toiled on, until the last source of support had vanished. The Quartermaster from whom she received work, having completed all the clothing he required, had no further use for her services, and she then saw nothing but a blank and dreary prospect, looming up before her. She had no means of purchasing food for her children. Piece by piece her furniture was sold to supply their wants, until nothing was left in the room but a solitary bedstead. Starvation in its worst form stared her in the face, until at last she sold what clothing she had brought out from New Orleans. This relieved her necessities but a short time, and then her last resource was gone.

If her present was dark, the future seemed but one black cloud of despair. Hope, that *ignis fatuus*, which deceives so many on earth, left the soldier's wife, and she was indeed wretched. The blooming woman had become a haggard and care-worn mother. She had no thought for herself. It was for her children alone she felt solicitous, and when the day arrived that saw her without the means of purchasing bread, her long filling cup of misery overflowed, and she wept.

Yes, she wept. Wept as if her whole life had been changed in a moment, from one of joy and happiness, to that of sadness and misery.

Her children in that dark hour clustered around her. *They* could not cry. A fast of over twenty-four hours had dried all tears within them. They only wondered for awhile, until the sharp pangs of hunger reminded them of another and greater woe. They too had been changed. The bloom of youth had departed from their little cheeks, while in the eyes of the oldest an unnatural light burned. She was fast sinking to the grave, but the mother knew it not. Knew not that her darling child had contracted a disease, which would shortly take her to Heaven, for the little Eva spoke no word of complaint. Young, as she was, she saw her mother's agony of soul, and though the little lips were parched and dry, she told not her ailing.

The tears continued to flow from Mrs. Wentworth, and still the children gazed on in wonderment. They knew not what they meant.

"Mother," at last said her little infant, "why do you cry?"

She took her on her knees. "Nothing, my darling," she replied.

"Then stop crying," he said, pressing his little hand on Mrs. Wentworth's cheek. "It makes me feel bad."

"I will stop crying, darling," she replied, drying her tears and smiling.

Smiles are not always the reply of the heart. We have seen men smile whoso whole life was a scene of misfortune, and yet this emblem of happiness has lit their features. It is outward show—a fruit, whose surface presents a tempting appearance to the eye, but which is blasted and withered within. Smiles are often like the fruit called the *Guava*. It is a beautiful looking fruit which grows in the West Indies, and to the taste is very luscious, but when examined through a microscope, it presents the appearance of a moving mass of worms. Its beauty is deceptive, nothing but a wretched view presents itself,

"Like dead sea fruit, that tempts the eye, And falls to ashes on the lips."

The child saw her mother smile, and the little heart forgot its hunger, and for a moment beat with joy. The gleam of sunshine that spread itself over him, did not last, for soon after the face of the mother assumed the same sad and cheerless expression, it had worn for many weeks. The child saw it, and again felt his hunger.

"Mother," she said, "give me a piece of bread."

"I will get some for you to-morrow," she replied. "There is no bread in the house this evening."

"I am *so* hungry," remarked the child. "Why is there no bread?"

"Mother has got no money to buy any," she replied.

The other child had remained quiet all the while. She still nestled to her mother's side and looked long and earnestly into her face. She was not thinking, for one of her years knew nothing of thought, but divined that all was not right with her mother.

"Eva, my child," the mother said, speaking to her for the first time, "go to the grocer's, and ask him if he will let me have a loaf of bread on credit."

"I am so glad you have sent for bread," exclaimed the infant on her knees, as he clapped his hand joyfully together.

Eva left the room, and in a few minutes returned empty handed.

"Has he refused to let you have it?" asked Mrs. Wentworth.

"Yes, mother," replied the child sadly. "He says he will not give credit to anybody."

"I thought as much," Mrs. Wentworth remarked.

"Then I won't get any bread?" asked the child on her knees.

"No, my darling," Mrs. Wentworth answered, "you must wait until to-morrow."

"I hav'nt eaten so long, mother," he said. "Why aint you got any bread?"

"Because mother is poor and without any money," she replied.

"But I feel so hungry," again the child remarked.

"I know it, my sweet boy," replied his mother, "but wait a little longer and I will give you something to eat."

Her heart was wrung with agony at the complaint of the child and his call for bread; but she knew not how to evade his questions or to procure food. The thought of asking charity had never once entered her mind, for those with whom she had daily intercourse, were too much engaged in self-interest to make her hope that any appeal for help would touch their sordid hearts; and yet food must be had, but how she knew not. Her promise to give her child food, on the next day, was made only to silence his call for bread. There was no prospect of receiving any money, and she could not see her children starve. But one recourse was left. She must sell the bed—the last piece of furniture remaining in the room—no matter that in so doing her wretchedness increased instead of diminished.

The child was not satisfied with her promise. The pangs he endured were too much for one of his age, and again he uttered his call for bread.

"There is no bread, Willy," said Eva, speaking for the first time. "Don't ask for any bread. It makes mamma sad."

The child opened his large blue eyes enquiringly upon his sister.

"My sweet, darling child," exclaimed Mrs. Wentworth, clasping the little Ella to her heart, and then bursting into tears at this proof of her child's fortitude, she continued: "Are you not hungry, too?"

"Yes, mother," she replied, "but"—Here the little girl ceased to speak as if desirous of sparing her mother pain.

"But what?" asked Mrs. Wentworth.

"Mother," exclaimed the child, throwing her arms round her mother's neck, and evading the question, "father will come back to us, and then we will not want bread."

The word "father," brought to Mrs. Wentworth's mind her absent husband. She thought of the agony he would endure if he knew that his wife and children were suffering for food. A swelling of her bosom told of the emotion raging within her, and again the tears started to her eyes.

"Come, my sweet boy," she said, dashing away the tears, as they came like dewdrops from her eyelids, and speaking to the infant on her knee, "it is time to go to bed."

"Aint I to get some bread before I go to bed?" he asked.

"There is none, darling," she answered hastily. "Wait until to-morrow and you will get some."

"But I am so hungry," again repeated the child, and again a pang of wretchedness shot through the mother's breast.

"Never mind," she observed, kissing him fondly, "if you love me, let me put you to bed like a good child."

"I love you!" he said, looking up into her eyes with all that deep love that instinct gives to children.

She undressed and put him to bed, where the little Ella followed him soon after. Mrs. Wentworth sat by the bedside until they had fallen asleep.

"I love you, mother, but I am so hungry," were the last words the infant murmured as he closed his eyes in sleep, and in that slumber forgot his agonizing pangs for awhile.

As soon as they were asleep, Mrs. Wentworth removed from the bedside and seated herself at the window, which she opened. There she sat, looking at the clouds as they floated by, dark as her own prospects were. The morning dawned and saw her still there. It was a beautiful morning, but the warble of the bird in a tree near by, as he poured forth his morning song, awoke no echo in the heart of the soldier's wife. All was cheerless within her. The brightness of the morning only acted like a gleam of light at the mouth of a cavern. It made the darkness of her thoughts more dismal.

CHAPTER THIRTEENTH.

THE APPEAL FOR CREDIT

The first call of the little boy, when he awoke in the morning, was for bread. He was doubly hungry now. Thirty-six hours had passed since he had eaten the last mouthful of food that remained in the room. Mrs. Wentworth on that night of vigils, had determined to make an appeal for help to the man she had purchased the furniture from, on her arrival at Jackson, and in the event of his refusing to assist her, to sell the bed on which her children were wont to sleep. This determination had not been arrived at without a struggle in the heart of the soldier's wife. For the first time in her life she was about to sue for help from a stranger, and the blood rushed to her cheeks, as she thought of the humiliation that poverty entails upon mortal. It is true, she was not about to ask for charity, as her object was only to procure credit for a small quantity of provisions to feed her children with. The debt would be paid, she knew well enough, but still it was asking a favor, and the idea of being obligated to a stranger, was galling to her proud and sensitive nature.

"Mother," exclaimed the child, as he rose from his bed, "it is morning now; aint I going to get some bread?"

"Yes," she replied, "I will go out to the shop directly and get you some."

About an hour afterwards she left the room, and bidding Ella to take care of her brother, while she was absent, bending her steps towards the store of Mr. Swartz. This gentleman had become, in a few short weeks, possessed of three or four times the wealth he owned when we first introduced him to our readers. The spirit of speculation had seized him among the vast number of the southern people, who were drawn into its vortex, and created untold suffering among the poorer classes of the people. The difference with Mr. Swartz and the great majority of southern speculators, was the depth to which he descended for the purpose of making money. No article of trade, however petty, that he thought himself able to make a few dollars by, was passed aside unnoticed, while he would sell from the paltry amount of a pound of flour to the largest quantity of merchandize required. Like all persons who are suddenly elevated, from comparative dependence, to wealth, he had become purse proud and ostentatious, as he was humble and cringing before the war. In this display of the mushroom, could be easily discovered the vulgar and uneducated favorite of frikle fortune. Even these displays could have been overlooked and pardoned, had he shown any charity to the suffering poor. But his heart was as hard as the flinty rocks against which wash the billows of the Atlantic. The cry of hunger never reached the inside of his breast. It was guarded with a covering of iron, impenetrable to the voice of misery.

And it was to this man that Mrs. Wentworth, in her hour of bitter need applied. She entered his store and enquired of the clerk for Mr. Swartz.

"You, will find him in that room," he replied, pointing to a chamber in the rear of the store.

Mrs. Wentworth entered the room, and found Mr. Swartz seated before a desk. The office, for it was his private office, was most elegantly furnished, and exhibited marks of the proprietor's wealth.

Mr. Swartz elevated his brows with surprise, as he looked at the care-worn expression and needy attire of the woman before him.

"Vot can I do for you my coot voman," he enquired, without even extending the courtesy of offering her a seat.

Mrs. Wentworth remained for a moment without replying. She was embarrassed at the uncourteous reception Mr. Swartz gave her. She did not recollect her altered outward appearance, but thought only of the fact that she was a lady. Her intention to appeal to him for credit, wavered for awhile, but the gaunt skeleton, WANT, rose up and held her two children before her, and she determined to subdue pride, and ask the obligation.

"I do not know if you recollect me," she replied at last, and then added, "I am the lady who purchased a lot of furniture from you a few weeks ago."

"I do not remember," Mr. Swartz observed, with a look of surprise. "But vot can I to for you dis morning?"

"I am a soldier's wife," Mrs. Wentworth commenced hesitatingly. "My husband is now a prisoner in the North, and I am here, a refugee from New Orleans, with two small children. Until a short time ago I had succeeded in supporting my little family by working on soldiers' clothing, but the Quartermaster's department having ceased to manufacture clothing, I have been for several days without work." Here she paused. It pained her to continue.

Mr. Swartz looked at her with surprise, and the idea came into his mind that she was an applicant for charity.

"Vell, vot has dat got to do vid your pisness," he observed in a cold tone of voice, determined that she should see no hope in his face.

"This much," she replied. "For over twenty-four hours my two little children and myself have been without food, and I have not a dollar to purchase it."

"I can't do anything for you," Mr. Swartz said with a frown.

"Dere is scarce a day but some peoples or anoder vants charity and I—"

"I do not come to ask for charity," she interrupted hastily. "I have only come to ask you a favor."

"Vat is it?" he enquired.

"As I told you before, my children and myself are nearly starving," she replied. "I have not the means of buying food at present, but think it more than likely I will procure work in a few days. I have called to ask if you would give me credit for a few articles of food until then, by which I will be able to sustain my family."

"I thought it vas something like charity you vanted," he observed, "but I cannot do vat you vish. It is te same ting every tay mit te sogers' families. Dey comes here and asks for charity and credit, shust as if a man vas made of monish.—Gootness gracious! I don't pelieve dat te peoples who comes here every tay is as pad off as tey vish to appear."

"You are mistaken, sir," Mrs. Wentworth replied, "if you think I have come here without being actually in want of the food, I ask you to let me have on credit. Necessity, and dire necessity alone, has prompted me to seek an obligation of you, and if you require it I am willing to pay double the amount you charge, so that my poor children are saved from starvation."

"I reckon you vill," Mr. Swartz said, "but ven you vill pay ish te question."

"I could not name any precise day to you," answered Mrs. Wentworth. "I can only promise that the debt will be paid. If I cannot even pay it myself, as soon as my husband is exchanged he will pay whatever you charge."

"Dat ish a very doubtful vay of doing pisness," he remarked. "I cannot do as you ask."

"Consider, sir," she replied. "The amount I ask you to credit me for is but small, and even if you should not get paid (which I am certain you will) the loss cannot be felt by a man of your wealth."

"Dat makes no differenish. I can't give you credit. It ish against my rules, and if I proke tem for you I vill have to do so for every body."

Mrs. Wentworth's heart sank within her at the determined manner in which he expressed his refusal. Without replying she moved towards the door, and was about to leave the room when she thought of the bedstead, on the sale of which she now depended. He may loan money on it she thought, and she returned to the side of his desk. He looked up at her impatiently.

"Vell," he remarked, frowning as he uttered the single word.

"As you won't give me credit," said Mrs. Wentworth, "I thought you may be willing to loan me some money if I gave a security for its payment."

"Vat kind of security?" he enquired.

"I have, at my room, a bedstead I purchased from you some time ago," she replied. "Will you lend a small sum of money on it?"

"No" he answered. "I am not a pawnbroker."

"But you might accommodate a destitute mother," remarked Mrs. Wentworth. "You have refused to give me credit, and now I ask you to loan me a small sum of money, for the payment of which I offer security."

"I cannot do it," he answered. "Ven I says a ting I means it."

"Will you buy the bedstead then?" asked Mrs. Wentworth in despair.

"Vat can I do mit it?" he enquired.

"Why you can sell again," replied Mrs. Wentworth. "It will always find a purchaser, particularly now that the price of everything has increased so largely."

"Veil, I vill puy te pedstead," he said, and then enquired: "How much monish do you vant for it?"

"What will you give me?" she asked.

"I vill give you forty tollars for it," he replied.

"It must be worth more than that," she remarked. "The price of everything is so increased that it appears to me as if the bedstead should command a higher price than that offered by you."

"Shust as you like, my goot voman," Mr. Swartz remarked, shrugging his shoulders. "If you vant at mine price, all veil and goot; if not, you can leave it alone. I only puy te piece of furniture to accommodate you, and you should pe tankful."

"I suppose I will be obliged to take your price," replied Mrs. Wentworth, "although I believe I could get more for it, did I know any one in town who purchased such things."

He made no reply, but calling his clerk ordered him to bring forty dollars from the safe. The clerk having brought the money retired, and left them alone again.

"Vere is te pedstead?" asked Swartz.

"It is at home," Mrs. Wentworth replied.

"Den you must pring it round here before I can pay for it," he observed.

"I am in want of the money now to buy bread," she answered. "If you will pay me and let your clerk follow with a dray, I would return home immediately and have the bedstead taken down and sent to you."

Mr. Swartz called the clerk again, and ordered him to bring a dray to the front of the store. The clerk did as he was requested, and soon after returned with the intelligence that the dray was ready.

"Do you follow dis voman to her house, and she vill give you a pedstead. Bring it down here," and then he added, speaking to the clerk who had not yet left the room: "Vat does te trayman sharge."

"One dollar and a half," was the reply.

Taking up the forty dollars which had been previously brought to him, Mr. Swartz counted out thirty-eight and a half dollars, and handed them to Mrs. Wentworth.

"De von tollar and a half out ish to pay for te trayage," he remarked as she received the money.

She made no reply, but left the room followed by the clerk, when, with the drayman, they soon arrived at her room. The bedstead was soon taken down and removed to Mr. Swartz's store.

"Sharge one huntred tollars for dat pedstead," he remarked to his clerk as soon as it had arrived.

While he was rejoicing at the good speculation he had made, the soldier's wife sat on a box in her room feeding her half famished children. The room was now utterly destitute of furniture, but the heart of the mother rejoiced at the knowledge that for a couple of weeks longer her children would have food.

CHAPTER FOURTEENTH.

DR. HUMPHRIES BUYS A SLAVE AND BRINGS HOME NEWS.

A few days after Mrs. Wentworth had sold her last piece of furniture, Dr. Humphries was walking along one of the principal streets in Jackson when he was stopped by a crowd that had gathered in front of an auction mart. On walking up he learned that it was a sheriff's sale of a "likely young negro girl." Remembering that Emma had requested him to purchase a girl as a waiting maid for her, he examined the slave and found her in all respects the kind of house servant he desired. Going up to the auctioneer who had just mounted a bench for the purpose of selling the slave, he enquired where she had come from. The auctioneer responded by handing the doctor a small hand bill setting forth the sale. After reading it he walked up to the slave and commenced to question her.

"What is your name?" he enquired.

"Elsy, sir," she replied.

"You say that you come from New Orleans," he continued.

"Yes, sir," she responded.

"What was your master's name?" asked the doctor.

"His name is Mr. Alfred Wentworth," the negro answered.

"Where is your master now?" he enquired, continuing his questions.

"Massa is a prisner in de Yankee army," she replied.

"And what made you leave New Orleans?" was the next question.

"My missis was turned away from de city, and I runaway from dem Yankees and come here to look for her."

"Have you not been able to find your mistress?" asked Dr. Humphries.

"No, sir. Jest as I came here de city police took me up and put me in jail."

"Excuse me," interrupted the auctioneer, "but I must sell this girl at once. Time is precious, so you must excuse me;" then turning to the crowd he continued: "Here is the slave, gentlemen. She is an intelligent looking negro, says she understands all that appertains to the duties of a house servant. What will you bid for her?"

"Seven hundred dollars," exclaimed a voice in the crowd.

"Thank you, sir; seven hundred dollars; going at seven hundred dollars. Look at the girl, gentlemen, going at seven hundred dollars. Can I get another bid?" exclaimed the auctioneer in the rapid voice peculiar to his class.

"Seven hundred and twenty-five," was the next bid.

"Seven hundred and fifty," Dr. Humphries cried out, having made up his mind to purchase her.

In a few minutes the slave was "knocked down" to the doctor for eleven hundred dollars, and after the proper form was gone through and the money paid, he ordered her to follow him, and retraced his steps homeward.

As our readers must have recognized already, Elsy was no other than the slave who was left at New Orleans by Mrs. Wentworth, and who declared that she would follow her mistress into the Confederate lines. After making several ineffectual attempts she had succeeded in reaching Baton Rouge, the capital of Louisiana, at which place she eluded the Federal pickets, and made her way to Jackson. The first part of her journey being through the country she passed unnoticed, until on her arrival at Jackson she was stopped by the police, who demanded her papers. Not having any she was confined in the county jail, and after due notice in the papers, calling for the owner to come and take her away, she was sold at auction according to law. The girl was very much grieved at her failure to find her mistress, but being of a good disposition soon became contented with her lot. Accordingly, when Dr. Humphries purchased her, she followed him home with a cheerful step.

On entering his house the doctor presented the negro to Emma.

"Here, Emma," he observed, "is a girl I have bought for you to-day."

"Thank you," she answered, looking at Elsy. "This is really a nice looking girl. Who did you buy her from?"

"She says she is from New Orleans. Her master is a prisoner in the hands of the Yankees, and her mistress being turned out of her home by Butler, is now somewhere in the Confederacy, but where, the girl cannot tell. When her mistress left New Orleans, the Yankees would not permit the slave to leave with her, but she succeeded in escaping from their lines, and came to Jackson, where she was arrested, and as no owner claimed her, she was sold to me at auction this morning according to law."

"Then we will not be doing justice to the owner of the girl, if we keep her constantly. Perhaps her mistress is some poor soldier's wife who would be glad to get the money you have expended, or may require her services."

"I have thought of that before I purchased her, but as she seems honest, I did not make the thought prevent me from getting her. I have also made up my mind to give her up should her owner at any time claim her, and he is a poor man."

"I am glad you have so decided," Emily replied, "for I should not have liked the idea of depriving any Confederate soldier of his slave, particularly if he is a poor man. And now," she continued, speaking to Elsy, "do you go in the next room and wait there until I come in."

Making a curtesy, Elsy left the parlor, and entered the room pointed out by Emily.

"I have some news for you, Emily," remarked the Doctor as soon as the negro had left the room.

"What is it about," she enquired.

"Something that will interest you considerably," he answered.

"If it will interest me, let me know what it is," she remarked.

"I have received a telegraphic dispatch from Harry," Dr. Humphries replied.

"Why, how could he have arrived in our lines?" she enquired, as a smile of joy illumined her features.

"Here is what the dispatch says:" "I arrived here this morning, having escaped from prison. Will be in Jackson on to-morrow's train. Show this to Emily."

"I am so glad," exclaimed Emily joyfully, as soon as her father had concluded reading the dispatch, "for," she continued, "I was beginning to be afraid that our unfortunate prisoners in the hands of the Yankees, would never be exchanged."

"You need not have labored under any such fear," Dr. Humphries observed. "The papers of this morning announce that a cartel has been arranged, and the prisoners held on both sides will be shortly exchanged."

"Nevertheless, I am glad that Harry has made his escape, for it will bring him to us sooner than we anticipated. Besides which, it is gratifying to know that he had no occasion to wait for an exchange."

"That is very true" replied her father, "and as he has safely escaped, you can rejoice, but the dangers which must have, necessarily presented themselves in the attempt, were of such a nature, that you would not have desired him to make the effort had you known them."

"He is safe, and we can well afford to laugh at them," she answered, "all I hope is that he may never be taken prisoner again."

"I do not believe he will relish the idea, much less the reality of such a thing again occurring," observed Dr. Humphries. "However," he continued, "he will be here to-morrow, and the little cloud that his capture had sent over our happiness, will have been removed, and all will again be bright."

As he concluded speaking, a servant entered with a letter containing a summons to attend a patient, and Dr. Humphries kissing his daughter once more, left the house.

CHAPTER FIFTEENTH.

ARRIVAL OF HARRY.

The next day Emily prepared herself to welcome the return of her lover, while Dr. Humphries proceeded to the railroad depot to meet him. In the meantime, we will give our readers a brief account of Harry's escape.

After leaving Chicago, Harry made his way through the country towards the Tennessee river. His journey was a dangerous one, for the people of Illinois where then highly elated at the successes which had attended the Yankee arms, and the few sympathisers that the South had in their midst, were afraid to express their sympathies. He, luckily, however, succeeded in finding out a worthy gentleman, who not only befriended him, but furnished the necessary means for his journey, and procured a passport for him to visit Nashville. Prepared for a continuation of his travel, Harry, who had been staying at the residence of his noble hearted host for three days, bade him adieu, and started on his way to Nashville. On arriving at Frankfort, Kentucky, he met with a man he had become acquainted with in Mississippi, but who, on account of his strong Union proclivities, was compelled to leave the South at the commencement of the war. This creature immediately recognized Harry, and knowing that he had always been an ardent Secessionist, conjectured that he was either a spy, or an escaped prisoner. Harry was accordingly arrested and carried before the military authorities, but his persistent denial of any knowledge of the man who had caused his arrest, and the passport he had received from the generous Illinoisan, induced the Yankee officer by whom he was examined, to release him, and permit his departure for Nashville.

Harry had many hair breadth escapes from detection and capture, but surmounting all the dangers which beset his path, he succeeded In reaching the Confederate lines in safety, and immediately started for Jackson. But one thing marred the joy he experienced at his daringly won freedom, and that was his ignorance of Alfred's fate. Had not the love of freedom been too strong his breast, he would have returned and endeavored to find his friend, but the success of his escape, and the idea that Alfred may have pursued a different road, deterred him from so doing. He determined, however, to make enquiry on his return to Jackson, whether his friend had arrived there, he having promised Harry to call on Dr. Humphries after they should arrive in the Confederate lines. He was not aware of the wound his friend had received, for though the Chicago papers made a notice of the attempted escape, and wounding of one of the prisoners, the notice was never seen by him, as he had no opportunity of getting a newspaper.

On arriving at Jackson, the evening after he had forwarded his telegraphic dispatch, Harry found Dr. Humphries at the depot awaiting his arrival. After they had exchanged hearty expressions of delight at meeting each other again, they proceeded to the house where Emma was anxiously looking out for her lover.

The customary salutations between lovers who have been separated being over, Harry proceeded to give an account of his escape, which was listened to with great interest by his hearers.

"By the way," he remarked, as soon as he had concluded, "has a soldier giving his name as Wentworth, and claiming to be a friend of mine, called here within the last ten days."

"No one has called here of that name," replied Dr. Humphries.

"I am very anxious to receive some intelligence of him," remarked Harry, "He was the friend I mentioned, having made my escape with."

"He may have taken a different road to the one you pursued," Dr. Humphries observed.

"If I were satisfied in my mind that he did escape safely, my fears would be allayed," he answered, "but," he continued, "we left the gates of the prison together, and were not four yards apart when the treachery of the guard was discovered. We both started at a full run, and almost instantaneously the Yankees, who lay in ambush for us, fired, their muskets in the direction we were going. The bullets whistled harmless by me, and I continued my flight at the top of my speed, nor did I discover the absence of my friend until some distance from the prison, when stopping to take breath, I called him by name, and receiving no answer found out that he was not with me. I am afraid he might have been shot."

"Did you hear no cry after the Yankees had fired," enquired Dr. Humphries.

"No, and that is the reason I feel anxious to learn his fate. Had he uttered any cry, I should be certain that he was wounded, but the silence on his part may have been caused from instant death."

"You would have, heard him fall at any rate; had he been struck by the Yankee bullets," remarked Dr. Humphries.

"That is very doubtful," he replied. "I was running at such a rapid rate, and the uproar made by the Yankees was sufficient to drown the sound that a fall is likely to create."

"I really trust your friend is safe," said Dr. Humphries. "Perhaps, after all, he did not make any attempt to escape, but surrendered himself to the Yankees."

"There is not the slightest chance of his having done such a thing," Harry answered. "He was determined to escape, and had told me that he would rather be shot than be re-captured, after once leaving the prison. I shall never cease to regret the misfortune should he have fallen in our attempt to escape. His kindness to me at Fort Donelson had caused a warm friendship to spring up between us. Besides which, he has a wife and two small children in New Orleans, who were the sole cause of his attempting to escape. He informed me that they were not in very good circumstances, and should Alfred Wentworth have been killed at Camp Douglas, God help his poor widow and orphans!"

"Did you say his name was Alfred Wentworth," inquired Emma, for the first time joining in the conversation.

"Yes, and do you know anything about him?" he asked.

"No," she replied, "I know nothing of the gentleman, but father bought a slave on yesterday, who stated that she has belonged to a gentleman of New Orleans, of the name you mentioned just now."

"By what means did you purchase her?" asked Harry addressing himself to Dr. Humphries.

The Doctor related to him the circumstances which occasioned the purchase, as well as the statement of Elsy. Harry listened attentively, for the friendship he felt for his friend naturally made him interested in all that concerned Alfred, or his family.

"Is there no way by which I can discover where Mrs. Wentworth is residing at present?" he enquired, after a moment of thought.

"None that I could devise," answered Dr. Humphries. "I know nothing of the family personally, nor would I have known anything of their existence, had not chance carried me to the auction sale, at which I purchased Elsy."

"Call the girl here for me," Harry said: "I must learn something more of the departure of Mrs. Wentworth and her children from New Orleans, and endeavor to obtain a clue to her whereabouts. It is a duty I owe to the man who saved my life, that everything I can do for his family shall be performed."

Emma left the room as he was speaking, and shortly after returned, followed by Elsy.

"Here is the girl," she said, as she entered.

"So you belonged to Mr. Wentworth of New Orleans, did you?" Harry commenced.

"I used to belong to him," replied Elsy.

"What made Mrs. Wentworth leave New Orleans?" he asked, continuing his questions.

Elsy gave a long account of the villainy of Awtry, in the usual style adopted by negroes, but sufficiently intelligible for Harry to understand the cause of Mrs. Wentworth being compelled to abandon her home, and take refuge in the Confederate lines.

"Did not your mistress state where she was going," he asked.

"No, sah," replied Elsy. "My mistis jest told me good bye when she left wid de children. I promised her I would get away from de Yankees, but she forgot to tell me whar she was gwine to lib."

"Did she bring out plenty of money with her?" he enquired.

"Yes, sah," Elsy answered. She had seen the sum of money possessed by Mrs. Wentworth, on her departure from New Orleans, and it being a much larger amount than she had ever beheld before, made the faithful girl believe that her mistress had left with quite a fortune.

"Very well, you can go now," remarked Harry. "It is a satisfaction," he continued as Elsy left the room, "to know that Wentworth's wife is well provided with money, although it does appear strange that she should have a plenty of funds, when her husband informed me, while in prison, that the money he left her with could not maintain his wife and children for any great length of time."

"She may have been furnished with money by some friend, who intending to remain in the city, had no use for Confederate Treasury notes," Dr. Humphries remarked.

"That is very likely, and I trust it is so," observed Harry, "However," he continued, "I shall take steps on Monday next, to find out where Mrs. Wentworth is now residing."

On Monday the following advertisement appeared in the evening papers:

INFORMATION WANTED.

Any one knowing where Mrs. Eva Wentworth and her two children reside, will be liberally rewarded, by addressing the undersigned at this place. Mrs. Wentworth is a refugee from New Orleans, and the wife of a gallant soldier, now a prisoner of war.

Jackson,——1862.

H. SHACKLEFORD.

It was too late. Extensively published as it was, Mrs. Wentworth never saw it. Her hardships and trials had increased ten-fold; she was fast drifting before the storm, with breakers before, threatening to wreck and sink into the grave the wife and children of Alfred Wentworth.

CHAPTER SIXTEENTH.

MR. ELDER DEMANDS HIS RENT.—NOTICE TO QUIT.

The money received by Mrs. Wentworth from Mr. Swartz, proved but a temporary relief for her children and herself. A fatal day was fast arriving, and she knew not how to avert the impending storm. By a great deal of labor and deprivation she had heretofore succeeded in paying the rent of the room she occupied, although Mr. Elder had twice advanced the price. Now there was no hope of her being able to obtain a sufficient sum of money to meet the demand of that gentleman, who would call on her the following day in person, did she not call at his office and settle for at least one months rent in advance. The month for which she had paid expired in three days, and she was apprehensive of being turned out, unless she could collect sufficient money to pay him. She knew not where to find the means. The room was stripped bare of furniture to supply the calls of nature; nothing but a mattress in one corner of the apartment, and a few cooking utensils remained. She labored day and night, to procure work, but all her efforts were unavailing. It appeared to her as if the Almighty had forsaken herself and children, and had left them to perish through want.

It cannot be that God would place his image on earth, and willingly leave them to perish from destitution. Many have been known to die of starvation, and the tales of wretchedness and woe with which the public ear is often filled attest the fact. Squalid forms and threadbare garments are seen, alas! too often in this civilised world, and the grave of the pauper is often opened to receive some unhappy mortal, whose life had been one scene of suffering and want. Philanthropy shudders and Christianity believes it to be a punishment, administered by the hand of God; that the haggard cause of the starved creature, who has thus miserably died, once contained the spirit of a mortal undergoing the penalty of Him, who judges mankind on high, and expiating through his heart-rending bodily agony, crimes committed in by-gone days.

This is not so in all cases. What mercy could we attribute to God, did he willingly entail misery upon the innocent, or punish them for the crimes of the guilty? Why call it a dispensation of Divine justice, that would condemn to weeks, months and years of wretchedness, the mortals he brought in the world himself? Who hath seen the hovel of the pauper; beheld its wretched inmates, heard their tale of woe, heard them tell of days passing without their having a crumb of bread to satisfy the cravings of hunger, or seen them in that last stage of destitution, when hunger brings on despair, until the mind wanders from its seat, and madness takes its place; heard the raving of the maniac, his frenzied call for bread, and his abject desolation, until death came kindly to relieve his sufferings, and felt not that the hand of God had never worked so much ill for his people? Is it profanity to say that the eye of God had wandered from them? We believe it; for the Book that teaches us of the Almighty, depicts him as a God of mercy and compassion. The eye of the Omnipotent is not upon the wretched. "He seeth all things," but there are times when His eyes are turned from those who endure the storm of a cold and heartless world, and He knows not of their suffering, until the Angel of Death brings their spirit before the Judgment seat.

God had not deserted the soldier's wife, but His eyes were turned away, and He saw not her condition. Thus was she left unaided by the hand of Providence. She felt her desolation, for as each day passed by, and her condition became worse, she knew that her prayers were unanswered. They reached not the ear of the Almighty, and the innocent children were allowed to participate of that bitter cup, which the chances of worldly fortune had placed before the unhappy family.

Three days sped away quickly, and the fatal morning arrived. She had no money to pay the rent, and the day passed away without Mr. Elder receiving a visit from her. She dared not to tell him of her position, but awaited patiently his arrival on the following day, for she well knew he would be sure to come.

The next morning saw him at her door, much annoyed at the trouble she gave him to call and collect the money. Mrs. Wentworth had nothing to say, nor had she a dollar to satisfy his demands.

"Good morning, madam," he said, as she opened the door to admit him, "I was much surprised at your not calling to pay the rent at my office on yesterday. I admire punctuality above everything else."

He entered the room, and cast his eyes on its empty walls. They did not satisfy him, for the absence of any furniture told the tale of the soldier's wife in a more graphic manner than words could have done.

"What does this mean?" he enquired.

"It means that necessity has compelled a mother to sacrifice everything to keep her children from starving," Mrs. Wentworth replied.

"Humph," said Mr. Elder. "This is singular. So I suppose," he continued, addressing her, "you will say you have no money to pay your month's rent in advance."

"I have not a dollar this day to buy bread," she answered.

A frown gathered on Mr. Elder's brow, as he remarked: "I suppose you recollect the arrangement made between us when you first hired the room from me."

"What arrangement was that?" she enquired in an absent manner.

"That on you failing to pay the rent, I should have the power to resume possession of the room, without giving you notice to leave."

"I recollect," she said.

"Well, in accordance with our arrangements, I shall require that you vacate the room to-day, as I can procure another tenant, who will be able to pay the rent promptly."

"Do you mean that I must leave to-day," she asked.

"Yes," he replied, "I desire to have the room renovated at once."

"Where can I go to without money," she enquired, in a tone more like as if she was addressing herself than speaking to him.

"I really cannot tell my good, woman," he answered, "I am sorry for your position, but cannot afford to lose the rent of my room, I am compelled to pay my taxes, and support myself by the money I receive from rent."

"I cannot leave to-day," Mrs. Wentworth cried in a despairing tone. "I cannot leave to-day. Oh, sir! look at my child lying on that wretched bed, and tell me, if you can have the heart to turn me out, homeless, friendless and alone."

"My good Woman," he answered. "I cannot help your misfortunes, nor can I do anything to assist you. If you can pay the rent, I have no objection to your remaining, but if you can not, I will be compelled to get another tenant who will be able."

"Sir," she remarked, speaking slowly. "I am a woman with two children, alone in this State. My husband and protector is now pining in a Yankee prison, a sacrifice on the altar of his country. Let me ask you as a man, and perhaps a father, to pause ere you turn a helpless woman from the shelter of your property. You appear wealthy, and the sum charged for the rent would make but little difference to you, if it was never paid. Oh! do not eject us from this room. My child lies there parched with fever, and to remove her may be fatal."

"There is no necessity for any appeals to me," he replied. "If I were to give way to such extravagant requests in your case, I should be necessitated to do so in others, and the result would be, that I should find myself sheltering all my tenants, without receiving any pay for house rent. The idea cannot be entertained for a moment."

"Let your own heart speak," she said, "and not the promptings of worldly thoughts. All those who rent your houses are not situated as I am. They are at home among friends, who will aid and succor them, if ever necessity overtook them. I am far away from home and friends. There is no one in this town that I can call upon for assistance, and even now, my children are without food for want of funds to purchase it. Do not add to my wretchedness by depriving them of shelter. Let me know that if we are to die of starvation, a roof, at least, will cover our bodies."

He looked at her with unchanged countenance. Not even the movement of a muscle, denoted that his heart was touched at her pathetic appeal. His expression was as hard and cold as adamantine, nor did a single feeling of pity move him. He cared for nothing but money; she could not give him what he wanted, and too sentiment of commiseration, no spark of charity, no feeling of manly regret at her sufferings entered his bosom.

"Be charitable," she continued. "I have prayed night after night to God to relieve my necessities; I have walked the town through and through in the effort to procure work, but my prayers have been unanswered, and my efforts have proven unavailing. At times the thought of the maelstrom of woe into which I am plunged, has well nigh driven me to madness. My brain has seemed on fire, and the shrieks of the maniac would have been heard resounding through the walls of this room, but my children would come before me, and the light of reason would again return. But for their sake I should welcome death as a precious boon. Life has but every charm for me. In the pale and alternated woman before you, none could recognize a once happy wife. Oh, sir!" she continued, with energy; "believe me when I tell you that for my children's sake alone, I now appeal. Hear me, and look with pity on a mother's pleadings. It is for them I plead. Were I alone, no word of supplication would you hear. I should leave here, and in the cold and turbid waters of Pearl river, find the rest I am denied on earth."

"This is a very unaccountable thing to me," said Mr. Elder. "You make an agreement to leave as soon as you fail to pay your rent, and now that that hour has arrived, instead of conforming to your agreement, I am beset with a long supplication. My good woman, this effort of yours to induce me to provide a home for your family at my expense, cannot be successful. You have no claim upon my charity, and those who have, are sufficiently numerous already without my desiring to make any addition. As I mentioned before, you must either find money to pay the rent, or vacate the room."

"Give me time," she said, speaking with an effort; "give me but two days, and I will endeavor either to obtain the money, or to procure somewhere to stay."

Mr. Elder knit his brows again as he answered. "I cannot give you two days, for I intend renting the room by to-morrow. You can, however, remain here until this evening, at which time you must either be prepared to leave, or find money to pay for the rent."

"It is well," she replied. "I will do as you say."

"Then you may expect me here this evening at dusk," he said, and turning towards the door left the room muttering; "when will I ever get rid of this crowd of paupers, who, it is always my luck to rent rooms to."

"God of Heaven aid me!" exclaimed Mrs. Wentworth, as she closed the door in the receding form of Mr. Elder, and sank on her knees before the bed on which Ella lay in a high fever.

CHAPTER SEVENTEENTH.

THE EJECTMENT

Mrs. Wentworth knew not where to go to procure money to pay the rent, and when she asked Mr. Elder to give her time to procure either the means of paying him, or to procure another place to stay, she did so only to avert the threatened ejectment for a brief period. Nor did she know where to procure another shelter. There was no one in the town that she knew from whom she could have obtained a room to rent, unless the money was paid in advance.

After Mr. Elder's departure, she fell on her knees and prayed for help, but she did so only from habit, not with the belief that an Omnipotent arm would be stretched out to aid her. There she knelt and prayed, until the thought of her sick child flashed across her brain, and rising, she stooped over and enquired how she felt.

"The same way," answered Ella. "I feel very hot, and my throat is quite parched."

"You have got the fever, darling," said Mrs. Wentworth.—"Is there anything I can do for you?"

"Nothing," replied Ella, "except," she continued, "you could get me something sweet to take this bitter taste from my mouth."

A pang shot through Mrs. Wentworth's heart as she replied, "I cannot get anything just now. You must wait until a little later in the day."

She spoke sadly, for it was a deception that she was practicing upon her child, when she promised to gratify her wishes at a later hour.

"Never mind," observed Ella. "Do not trouble yourself, my dear mother, I do not want it very badly."

The little girl defined the cause of her mother's not acceding to her request at that moment, and she had no desire to cause her additional pain, by again asking for anything to moisten her parched lips, or remove the dry and bitter taste that the fever had caused.

Mrs. Wentworth had at last found out that Ella was sick.—Not from any complaint of the child, for the little girl remained suffering in silence, and never hinted that she was unwell.—But she had become so weak that one morning, on endeavoring to rise from the bed, she fell back and fainted from exhaustion, and on her mother's chafing her forehead with water for the purpose of reviving her, discovered that Ella had a hot fever. She was very much alarmed, and would have called a doctor, but knowing no medical man who would attend her child without remuneration, she was necessitated to content herself with what knowledge she had of sickness. This had caused the money she had remaining in her possession to be quickly expended.

The little girl bore her illness uncomplainingly, and although each day she sunk lower and felt herself getting weaker, she concealed her condition, and answered her mother's questions cheerfully. She was a little angel that God had sent to Mrs. Wentworth. She was too young to appreciate the extent of her mother's wretchedness, but she saw that something was wrong and kept silent, and she lay there that day sick. There was no hope for the child. Death had marked her as his prey, and nothing could stay or turn away his ruthless hand from this little flower of earth. Stern fate had decreed that she should die. The unalterable sentence had been registered in the book of Heaven, and an angel stood at her bedside ready to take her to God.

The day passed over the wretched family. Ella lay on the bed in silence throughout, what appeared to her, the long and weary hours; the little boy called every few minutes for bread, and as his infant voice uttered the call, the agony of Mrs. Wentworth increased. Thus was the day passed, and as the dusk of evening spread its mantle over the town, the soldier's wife prepared to receive her summons for ejectment. She was not kept waiting long. No sooner had the darkness set in, than Mr. Elder, accompanied by another man, opened the door and entered the room.

"Well," he said, "have you succeeded in procuring money to pay the rent."

"I have not," Mrs. Wentworth answered.

"I suppose you have made arrangements to go somewhere else then," he remarked.

"No," she replied. "My child has been ill all day long, and I was compelled to remain here and attend to her wants."

"That is very unfortunate," Mr. Elder remarked, "for this gentleman," pointing to the stranger who accompanied him, "has made arrangements to take the room, and will move into it to-night.".

"Will he not wait until the morning," she enquired.

"I do wot know," he replied. "Will you," he asked, speaking to the man, "be willing to wait until to-morrow before you take possession?"

"Bo jabers! I've got to leave my owld room to-night, and if I cannot git this I must take another that I can get in town," answered the man, who was a rough and uneducated son of the Emerald Isle.

"That settles the matter, then," observed Mr. Elder. "You will have to leave," he continued, addressing Mrs. Wentworth. "You will perceive that I cannot lose a tenant through your remaining in the room to-night."

"Och!" said the Irishman, "if the lady can't lave to-night, shure ah' I will take the other room, for be jabers I wouldn't have a woman turned out of doors for me."

"You need not fear about that, my good friend," remarked Mr. Elder. "Does the room suit you?"

"Yes! It does well enough for myself and my children," was the answer.

"Then you can consider yourself a tenant from to-night," Mr. Elder said. "Go and bring your things here. By the time you return I shall have the room vacated and ready for you."

"Jist as you say, yer honor," replied the man, as he bowed himself from the room.

"And now, my good woman," remarked Mr. Elder, "you will perceive the necessity of removing your children and whatever articles you may have here to some other place at once. I cannot be induced to grant any further time, and lose tenants by the operation."

"Great God, sir!" exclaimed Mrs. Wentworth, "where am I to go to? I know of no place where I can find a shelter this night. You cannot, must not, force me to leave."

"I trust you will not put me to the necessity of having you ejected by force," remarked Mr. Elder. "You are fully aware that by the arrangement entered into between us, when you first rented the room, that I am doing nothing illegal in requiring you to leave. You will save me both trouble and pain by doing as I have requested."

"I cannot," she replied, pressing her hands to her forehead, and then bursting into tears she exclaimed appealingly: "For the sake of God have pity, sir! Let not your heart be so hardened, but turn and befriend a soldiers wretched wife. There is scarce a beast but contains some touch of feeling, scarce a heart but vibrates in some degree, and beats with a quicker pulsation at the sight of poverty and misery. Let me hope that yours contains the same feeling, and beats with the same sorrow at the miserable scene before you. Look around you, sir, and see the destitution of my family; go to the side of that lowly bed and press your hand upon the burning brow of my child; call that little boy and ask him how long he has been without food, look at a wretched mother's tears, and lot a gracious God remove the hardness from your heart, and drive us not homeless from this roof. Think not that the ragged, woman who now stands before you, weeping and pleading, would have thus supplicated without a cause. There was a time when I never dreamed of experiencing such suffering and hardship, such bitter, bitter woe. Oh! sir, let pity reign dominant in your heart."

He was unmoved. Why should he care for the misery of strangers? Was he not of the world as man generally finds it? The exceptions to the rule are not of this earth. They occupy a place in the celestial realms, for, if even they may have committed sins in early life, their deeds of charity blots out the record, and they enter Heaven welcomed by the hosts of angels who dwell there, while their absence from this creates a void not easily filled.

Mr. Elder answered her not for several minutes. He stood there with his arms folded, silently gazing upon the thin form of Mrs. Wentworth, who, with clasped hands and outstretched arms, anxiously awaited his decision. But he gave no promise of acquiescence, no hope of pity, no look of charity in his features—they looked cold, stern, and vexed.

There she stood the picture of grief, awaiting the words that would either give her hope or plunge her forever into the fathomless depths of despair. The eyes of the soldier's wife were turned on Mr. Elder with a sad and supplicating look. In any other but the cold, calculating creature before her, their look might have moved to pity, but with him nothing availed; not even a struggle for mastery between humanity and brutality could be seen, and as she gazed upon him she felt that there was no chance of her wishes being gratified.

Her little son clung to her dress half frightened at the attitude of his mother, and the stern and unforbidding aspect of Mr. Elder. Ella strove to rise while her mother was speaking, but fell back on her bed unable to perform the effort. She was, therefore, content to be there and listen to the conversation as it occurred between Mr. Elder and her mother. Her little heart was also tortured, for this had been the first time she had ever heard such passionate and earnest language as was depicted in Mrs. Wentworth's words.

At last Mr. Elder spoke, and his words were eagerly listened to by Mrs. Wentworth.

"This annoys me very much," he said. "Your importunities are very disagreeable to me, and I must insist that they shall cease. As I told you before, I cannot afford to lose tenants in an unnecessary act of liberality, and through mistaken charity. The fact is," he continued in a firm and decisive tone, "you *must* leave this room to-night. I will not listen to any more of your pleading. Your case is but the repetition of many others who fled from their homes and left all they had, under the impression that the people of other States would be compelled to support them. This is a mistaken idea, and the sooner its error is made known the better it will be for the people of the South, whose homes are in the hands of the enemy."

"Then you are determined that my children and myself shall be turned from the shelter of this room to-night," she enquired, dropping her hands by her side, and assuming a standing attitude.

"You have heard what I have already said, my good woman," he replied. "And let me repeat, that I will listen to no further supplications."

"I shall supplicate to you no more," she answered. "I see, alas! too well, that I might sooner expect pity from the hands of an uncivilized Indian than charity or aid from you. Nor will I give you any trouble to forcibly eject me."

"I am very glad to hear it," he rejoined.

"Yes," she continued, without noticing his words, "I shall leave of my own accord, and there," she said, pointing to Ella, "lies my sick child. Should exposure on this night cause her death, I shall let you know of it that you may have some subject, accruing from your heartless conduct, on which to ponder."

Slowly she removed all the articles that were in the room, and placed them on the sidewalk. There were but few things in the room, and her task was soon completed.

"Come, darling," she said as she wrapped up Ella in a cover-lid and lifted the child in her arms, "come, and let us go."

Mr. Elder still stood with folded arms looking on.

"Farewell, sir," she said, turning to him, "you have driven a soldier's helpless wife and children from the roof that covered them into the open streets, with none other than skies above as a covering. May God pardon you as I do," and speaking to the little boy who still clung to her dress, she replied, "Come, darling, let us go."

Go where? She knew not, thought not where. She only knew that she was now homeless.

The clouds looked as serene, the stars twinkled as merrily as ever, and the moon shed as bright a light upon the form of the soldier's wife, as she walked out of that room, a wanderer upon the earth, as it did on scenes of peace and happiness. The Ruler of the Universe saw not the desolate mother and her children; thus there was no change in the firmament, for had He gazed upon them at that moment, a black cloud would have been sent to obscure the earth, and darkness would have taken the place of light.

CHAPTER EIGHTEENTH.

THE RESTING PLACE—ANOTHER VISIT TO MR. SWARTZ.

The mother and her child walked on in silence. Mrs. Wentworth knew not where to go. From her heart the harrowing cry of desolation went out, and mingled with the evening air, filling it with the sound of wretchedness, until it appeared dull and stifling. But she knew not this, for to her it had never appeared pleasant. For weeks past her cup of misery had been filling, and as each drop of sorrow entered the goblet of her life, so did all sense of what was happy and lovely depart from her heart. She was, indeed, a breathing figure of all that could be conceived miserable and unhappy. The flowers that bloomed in the Spring time of her happy years, had withered in the winter of her wretched weeks, and over the whole garden of her life, nothing but the dead and scentless petals remained, to tell of what was once a paradise of affection—a blooming image of love.

As she walked on she discovered that the child she carried in her arms had fainted. She paused not for consideration, but observing a light in a small cabin near by, she hurriedly bent her steps towards it, and entered through the half opened door. It was the home of an aged negro woman, and who looked up much surprised at the intrusion.

"Here, auntie," Mrs. Wentworth said hastily, "give me some water quickly, my child has fainted."

"Goodness, gracious, what could ha' made you bring dem children to dis part of de town dis time o' night," exclaimed the old negress, as she hastened to do the bidding of Mrs. Wentworth, who had already placed the inanimate body of Ella on the negro's humble bed.

The water being brought, Mrs. Wentworth sprinkled it upon the face of the child, but without avail. Ella still remained motionless, and to all appearances lifeless.

"Great Heaven!" exclaimed Mrs. Wentworth, "my child cannot be dead!"

"Top a bit, mistis, an' I will fix de little gal for you," said the old negro, hobbling, to the bedside, with a small bottle filled with camphor in her hand. "Dis stuff will bring her to. Don't be afeard, she ain't dead."

Pouring out some of the stimulant in one hand, the kind-hearted old woman bathed Ella's face with it, and held the bottle to her nostrils, until a sigh from the child showed that she still lived. After a few seconds she opened her eyes, and looked up to her mother, who was, bending with anxious countenance over her.

"Dar now," said the old negro in a tone of satisfaction, "did not I tell you dat de sweet little child was libbing."

"Thank you, old woman, God in Heaven bless you!" exclaimed Mrs. Wentworth, as she clapped the old woman's hand in her own.

"Berry well, berry well," was the answer of the negro, "you welcome misses."

There, in the cabin of that good old slave, the soldier's wife heard the first voice of kindness that had greeted her ears for months. From the hands of a servile race she had received the first act of charity, and in a land like this. In the performance of that kindness, the old slave had done more to elevate herself than all the philanthropists and abolitionists of the North could have done. Could the cursed race, whose war upon the South have seen this act, they would have conceded to her people the justice of their right to slavery, when such a slave as this existed.

"What make you come to dis part ob town to-night, missis," asked the negro, after a few moments of silence.

"Nothing, nothing, my good woman," replied Mrs. Wentworth hastily. She could not let a slave know of her trials and misery.

"Poh ting!" ejaculated the old woman in a compassionate tone, but too low for Mrs. Wentworth to hear her. "I 'spec her husband been treatin' her bad. Dem men behave berry bad sometime," and with a sigh she resumed her silence.

The soldier's wife sat by the bedside, on one of the rude chairs, that formed a portion of the furniture, and remained plunged in thought. A deep sleep had overtaken Ella, although her breathing was heavy, and the fever raged with redoubled violence.

"Mother can't I get something to eat?" asked her little son. His words woke his mother from her thoughts, but before she could reply, the old negro had forestalled.

"Is it some ting you want to eat, my little darling," she enquired, rising from her seat, and going to a little cupboard near the door of the room.

"Yes granny," he answered, "I am quite hungry."

"Bress your little heart," she remarked, giving him a large piece of bread. "Here is some ting to eat."

Taking the child on her knees, she watched him until he had completed eating the food, when putting him down, she opened a trunk, and pulled out a clean white sheet, which she placed on a little mattress near the bed.

"Come now," she said, "go to bed now like a good boy."

The child obeyed her, and was soon enjoying a refreshing sleep.

"Where will you sleep to-night, auntie," asked Mrs. Wentworth, who had been a silent observer of the old woman's proceedings.

"I got some tings 'bout here; missis, dat will do for a bed," she answered.

"I am sorry I have to take away your bed to-night," remarked Mrs. Wentworth, "but I hope I will be able to pay you for your kindness some time."

"Dat's all right," replied the old negress, and spreading a mass of different articles on the floor, she crept in among them, and shortly after fell asleep, leaving Mrs. Wentworth alone with her thoughts, watching over the sleeping forms of her children.

The next morning the old woman woke up early, and lighting fire, made a frugal but amply sufficient breakfast, which, she placed before her uninvited guests. Mrs. Wentworth partook of the meal but slightly, and her little son ate heartily. Ella being still asleep, she was not disturbed. Shortly after the meal was over, the old negro left the cabin, saying she would return some time during the day.

About nine o'clock, Ella woke, and feebly called her mother. Mrs. Wentworth approached the bedside, and started back much shocked at the appearance of her child. The jaws of the little girl had sunk, her eyes were dull and expressiveless and her breath came thick and heavily.

"What do you wish my darling," enquired her mother.

"I feel quite sick, mother," said the little girl, speaking faintly and with great difficulty.

"What is the matter with you?" Mrs. Wentworth asked, her face turning as pale as her child's.

"I cannot breathe," she answered, "and my eyes feel dim. What can be the matter?"

"Nothing much, my angel," replied her mother. "You have only taken a cold from exposure in the air last night. Bear up and you will soon get well again."

"I feel so different now from what I did before," she remarked. "Before I was so hot, and now I feel as cold as ice."

Mrs. Wentworth put her hand upon the face of her child. It was indeed as cold as ice, and alarmed the mother exceedingly. She knew not how to act; she was alone in the cabin, and even had the old negro been at home, she had no money to purchase medicines with. She was determined, however, that something should be done for her child, and the thought of again appealing to Mr. Swartz for assistance came into her mind.

"Perhaps, he will loan me a small sum of money when he learns how destitute I am, and that my child is very ill," she said musingly, and then added: "At any rate I will try what I can do with him."

Turning to Ella Mrs. Wentworth said: "Do you think you could remain here with your brother until my return. I want to go out and get something for you to take."

"Yes, mother, but do not be long," she replied. "I will try and keep brother by me while you are away."

"Very well," said Mrs. Wentworth, "I shall make haste and return."

Admonishing her little son not to leave the room during her absence, Mrs. Wentworth was on the point of leaving the room when Ella called to her: "Be sure to come back soon, mother," she said. "I want you back early particularly."

"Why, my darling?" enquired her mother.

"Why, in case I should be going to—" Here her voice sunk to a whisper, and her mother failed to catch what she said.

"In case you should be going to, what?" enquired Mrs. Wentworth.

"Nothing, mother," she replied. "I was only thinking, but make haste and come back."

"I will," her mother answered, "I will come back immediately."

Choking the sob that rose in her throat, Mrs. Wentworth left the room and proceeded towards Mr. Swartz's office. Her visit was a hopeless one, but she determined to make the trial. She could not believe that the heart of every man was turned against the poor and helpless.

What a world is this we live in! We view with calm indifference the downfall of our fellow-mortals. We see them struggling in the billows of adversity, and as our proud bark of wealth glides swiftly by, we extend no helping hand to the worn swimmer. And yet we can look upon our past life with complacency, can delight to recall the hours of happiness we have past, and if some scene of penury and grief is recalled to our memory, we drive away the thought of what we then beheld and sought not to better.

What is that that makes man's heart cold as the mountain tops of Kamtschatka? It is that cursed greed for gain—that all absorbing ambition for fortune—that warps the heart and turns to adamant all those attributes of gentleness with which God has made us. The haggard beggar and the affluent man of the world, must eventually share the same fate. No matter that on the grave of the first—"no storied urn records who rests below," while on the grave of the other, we find in sculptured marble long eulogies of those who rest beneath, telling us "not what he was, but what he should have been." Their end is the same, for beneath the same sod they "sleep the last sleep that knows no waking," and their spirits wing their flight to the same eternal realms, there to be judged by their own merits, and not by the station they occupied below.

If there are men in this world who cannot be changed by wealth, Swartz was not of the number. What cared he for the sighs of the desolate, the appeals of the hungry, or the tears of the helpless? His duty was but to fill his coffers with money, and not to expend it in aimless deeds of charity. He looked upon the poor just as we would look upon a reptile—something to be shunned.

It was indeed a wild hallucination that induced Mrs. Wentworth to bend her steps towards his office. Could he have seen her as she was coming, he would have left his room, for the sight of the mendicant filled him with greater horror than a decree of God declaring that the end of the world had come.

CHAPTER NINETEENTH.

AN ACT OF DESPAIR.

Mrs. Wentworth reached the store of Mr. Swartz and entered. The clerk looked at her in astonishment. She was unrecognizable. Her dress was ragged and dirty; the hands and face that once rivalled the Parian marble in whiteness, were tanned by toil, and lay shrivelled and dried. Her hair was dishevelled and gathered up in an uncomely heap on the back of her head. She looked like the beggar, she had become.

"Some beggar," the clerk said, in a contemptuous tone, as he advanced towards her.

"Is Mr. Swartz in?" enquired Mrs. Wentworth in a husky tone.

"What do you want with him?" he demanded in a gruff voice.

"I desire to see him privately, for a few moments," she answered.

"If it is charity you have come to beg, you may as well save yourself the trouble," observed the clerk. "This house don't undertake to support all the beggars in Jackson."

As his brutal words fell on her ear, a spark of womanly dignity filled her breast, and her eyes kindled with indignation. She looked at him for a moment sternly and silently, until her gaze caused him to turn his countenance from her, abashed at the mute rebuke she had administered. The pride of by-gone days had returned, with the unfeeling remarks of the clerk, and Mrs. Wentworth again felt all the bitterness of her position.

"I did not say I was an applicant for charity," she said at last "All I desire to know is, if Mr. Swartz is in."

"I believe he is," replied the clerk. "Do you wish to see him, ma'am."

His tone was more respectful. Even poverty can command respect at times, and the threadbare garment be looked upon with as much difference as the gorgeous silken dress. It was so at this moment.

"Yes, I desire to see him," answered Mrs. Wentworth. "Be kind enough to inform Mr. Swartz that a lady has called upon him."

As she used the word "lady," the clerk elevated his eyebrows, and a smile of pity stole over his features. Lady! Could the miserable looking object, who stood before him have any claim to the title. Poor woman! She knew not that the outward form of woman is the only recognized title to the term. What though the mind be filled with the loftiest sentiment, and stored with the richest lore of learning. What though the heart be purer than the snow which covers the mountain tops, can they ever claim a position among the favorites of fortune, when accompanied by beggary? Philanthropists, and philosophers tell us they can, but the demon, Prejudice, has erected a banner, which can never be pulled down, until man resumes the patriarchal life of centuries ago, and society, the mockery by which we claim civilization was built up, is removed from the earth, and mankind can mingle with each other in free and unrestricted intercourse.

That day will never come.

But to return to our story. The clerk looked pityingly at Mrs. Wentworth for a moment, then walked to the door of Mr. Swartz's office, and knocked.

The door was opened.

"There is a *lady* here who wants to see you on private business," he said with emphasis.

"Shust tell de lady I will see her in a few minutes," replied the voice of Mr. Swartz, from the interior of the room.

The clerk withdrew, after closing the door, and advanced to where Mrs. Wentworth was standing.

"Mr. Swartz will see you in a few moments, he said."

"Go back for me, and tell him my business is urgent, and will admit of no delay," she answered.

Her thoughts were of the little girl, who lay ill on the bed in the negro's cabin, and to whom she had promised to return quickly.

The clerk withdrew, and announced her wishes, to his employer.

"Vell," said Mr. Swartz. "Tell her to come in."

She walked up to the door, and as she reached the threshold it opened and Mr. Elder, stood before her. She spoke not a word as he started from surprise at her unexpected appearance. She only gazed upon him for awhile with a calm and steady gaze. Hastily dropping his eyes to the ground, Mr. Elder recovered his usual composure, and brushing past the soldier's wife left the store, while she entered the office where Mr. Swartz was.

"Oot tam," he muttered as she entered. "I shall give dat clerk te tevil for sending dis voman to me. Sum peggar I vill pet."

"I have called on you again, Mr. Swartz," Mrs. Wentworth began.

Mr. Swartz looked at her as if trying to remember where they had met before, but he failed to recognize her features.

"I don't know dat you vash here to see me pefore," he replied.

"You do not recognize me," she remarked, and then added: "I am the lady who sold her last piece of furniture to you some time ago."

He frowned as she reminded him who she was, for he then surmised what the object of her visit was.

"Oh!" he answered, "I recollect you now, and vat do you vant?"

"I have come upon the same errand," she replied. "I have come once more to ask you to aid me, but this time come barren of anything to induce you to comply with my request. Nothing but the generous promptings of your heart can I hold up before you to extend the charity I now solicit."

"You have come here to peg again," he observed, "but I cannot give you anything. Gootness! ven vill te place pe rid of all te peggers?"

"I cannot help my position," she said. "A cruel fortune has deprived my of him who used to support me, and I am now left alone with my children to eke out the wretched existence of a pauper. Last night I was turned out of my room by the man who left here a few seconds ago, because I could not pay for my rent. One of my children was sick, but he cared not for that. I told him of my poverty, and he turned a deaf ear towards me. I was forced to leave, and my child has become worse from exposure in the night air."

"And vot have I cot to do mit all dis," he enquired.

"You can give me the means of purchasing medicine for my sick child," she replied. "The amount thus bestowed cannot cause you any inconvenience, while it may be the means of saving life."

"Dis never vill do," Mr. Swartz said, interrupting her. "My goot woman, you must go to somepody else, I can't give away my monish."

"You have got a plenty," she persisted, "you are rich. Oh, aid me! If you believe there is a God above, who rewards the charitable, aid me, and receive the heartfelt blessings of a mother. Twenty dollars will be enough to satisfy my present wants, and that sum will make but little difference to a man of your wealth."

"Mine Cot!" he exclaimed, "If I make monish I work for it, and don't go about begging."

"I know that," she answered, "and it is to the rich that the poor must appeal for assistance. This has made me come to you this day. Let my desire be realized. Aid me in saving the life of my child who is now lying ill, and destitute of medical attendance."

He could not appreciate her appeal, and he again refused.

"I can't give you any ding," he answered.

"There is a virtue which shines far more than all the gold you possess," replied Mrs. Wentworth. "It is in man what chastity is in a woman. An act of charity ennobles man more than all the fame bestowed upon him for any other merit, and his reward is always commensurate with his works. Let this virtue move you. The ear of God cannot always be turned against my prayers to Him, and the hour must surely come, when my husband will be released from prison, and be enabled to repay any kindness you may show his wife and children. Let me have the money I have asked you for." "Oh, sir!" she continued, falling on her knees before him, "believe the words I speak to you, and save my child from the hands of death. But a short time ago I left her gasping for breath, with cold drops of perspiration resting on her brow, perhaps the marks of approaching dissolution. She is very ill, and can only recover through proper treatment. Place it in my power to call a physician and to procure medicines, and I shall never cease to bless you."

He moved uneasily in his chair, and averted his head from where she was kneeling, not because he felt touched at her appeal, but because he felt annoyed at her importuning him for money.

"Here my voman," he said at last. "Here is von tollar pill, dat is all I can give you."

She looked at the note in his extended hand, and felt the mockery.

"It will not do," she answered. "Let me have the amount I have asked you for. You can spare it. Do not be hardened. Recollect it is to provide medicine for the sick."

"I can't do it," he replied. "You should be shankful for what you get."

His motive in offering her the dollar, was not from a charitable feeling, it was only to get rid of a beggar.

"Oh God!" she groaned, rising from her knees, and resting her elbow on an iron safe near by. "Have you a heart?" she exclaimed wildly, "I tell you my child is ill, perhaps at this moment dying, aid me! aid me! Do not turn away a miserable mother from your door to witness her child die through destitution, when it is in your power to relieve its sufferings, and save it, so that it may live to be a blessing and solace to me. If not for my sake, if not for the sake of the child, let me appeal to you for charity, for the sake of him, who is now imprisoned in a foreign dungeon. He left me to defend you from the enemy—left his wife and children to starve and suffer, for the purpose of aiding in that holy cause we are now engaged in conflict for. For his sake, if for no other, give me the means of saving my child."

He did not reply to her passionate words, but simply rang a bell that stood on the table before which he was seated. His clerk answered the summons.

"If you vont quit mithout my making you," he observed to Mrs. Wentworth in a brutal tone, "I must send for a police officer to take away. Gootness," he continued, speaking to himself, "I pelieve te voman is mat."

"Save yourself the trouble," she replied, "I will leave. I am not yet mad," she added. "But, oh, God! the hour is fast approaching when madness must hold possession of my mind. I go to my child—my poor dying child. Oh, Heaven, help me!"

As she moved her hand from the safe, she perceived a small package of money lying on it. She paused and looked around. The clerk had withdrawn at a sign from Mr. Swartz, while that gentleman was gazing intently at the open pages of a ledger, that lay before him. For a moment she hesitated and trembled from head to foot, while the warm blood rushed to her cheeks, until they were a deep crimson hue. Swiftly she extended her hand towards the package, and grasped it; in another instant it was concealed in her dress, and the act of despair was accomplished.

"God pity me!" she exclaimed, as she left the room and departed from the scene of her involuntary crime.

Despair had induced her to commit a theft, but no angel of God is purer in mind than was the Soldier's Wife, when she did so. It was the result of madness, and if the Recording Angel witnessed the act, he recorded not the transgression against her, for it was a sin only in the eyes of man; above it was the child of despair, born of a pure and innocent mind, and there is no punishment for such.

"Thank God, I have the means of saving my darling child," exclaimed Mrs. Wentworth, as she bent her steps towards a druggist's store. Entering it, she purchased a few articles of medicine, and started for the old negro's cabin, intending to send the old woman for a physician, as soon as she could reach there.

Swiftly she sped along the streets. Many passers by stopped and looked with surprise at her rapid walking. They knew not the sorrows of the Soldier's Wife. Many there were who gazed upon her threadbare habiliments and haggard features, who could never surmise that the light of joy had ceased to burn in her heart. Their life had been one long dream of happiness, unmarred, save by those light clouds of sorrow, which at times flit across the horrizon of man's career, but which are swiftly driven away by the sunshine of happiness, or dissipated by the gentle winds of life's joyous summer.

And the crowds passed her in silence and surprise, but she heeded them not. Her thoughts were of the angel daughter in the negro's lonely cabin. To her she carried life; at least she thought so, but the inevitable will of Death had been declared. Ella was dying.

The eye of God was still turned from the widow and her children. He saw them not, but his Angels, whose duty it is to chronicle all that occurs on earth, looked down on that bright autumn day, and a tear fell from the etherial realms in which they dwelt, and rested upon the Soldier's Wife.

It was the tear of pity, not of relief.

CHAPTER TWENTIETH

THE DYING CHILD.

After the departure of Mrs. Wentworth, the little girl lie still upon the bed, while her little brother played about the room. Nearly one hour elapsed in silence. The breath of the child became shorter and harder drawn. Her little face became more pinched, while the cold drops of perspiration rose larger on her forehead. Instinct told her she was dying, but young as she was, death created no terrors in her heart. She lay there, anxious for her mother's return, that she may die in the arms of the one who gave her birth. Death seemed to her but the advent to Heaven, that home in which we are told all is goodness and happiness. She thought herself an Angel dwelling with the Maker, and in her childish trustfulness and faith almost wished herself already numbered among the Cherubs of Paradise.

The old negro returned before Mrs. Wentworth, and walking to the bedside of the child, looked at her, and recognized the impress of approaching death. She felt alarmed, but could not remedy the evil. Looking at the child sorrowfully for a moment, she turned away.

"Poh chile," she muttered sadly, "she is dyin' sho' and her mammy is gone out. Da's a ting to take place in my room."

"Granny," said Ella feebly.

"What do you want my darlin' chile," answered the old woman, returning to the bedside.

"See if mother is coming," she requested.

The old woman walked to the door, and looked down the street. There was no sign of Mrs. Wentworth.

"No missy," she said to Ella, "your mammy is not coming yet."

"Oh, I do wish she would come," remarked the little girl.

"Lie still, darlin'," the old woman answered. "Your mammy will come back directly."

The child lay still for several minutes, but her mother came not and she felt that before many hours she would cease to live.

"Look again, granny, and see if mother is coming," she again requested, and in a fainter tone.

The old woman looked out once more, but still there was no sign of Mrs. Wentworth.

"Neber mind, darlin' your mammy will cum directly," she said, and then added. "Let me know what you want and I will git it for you."

"I don't want anything, granny," Ella answered, and remained silent for a moment, when she continued: "Granny aint I going to die?"

The old negro looked at her for a moment, and a tear stole down her withered features. She could not answer, for ignorant and uneducated as she was, the signs which betoken the parting of the soul from the body, were too apparent, not to be easily recognized.

"Poh chile," she muttered, as she turned her head and brushed away the falling tear.

"Answer me, granny," said Ella. "I am not afraid to die, but I would like to bid mother good-bye, before I went to Heaven."

"Don't tink of sich tings chile'" observed the old woman. "You is sick now only; lie still and you will soon see your mother."

The time sped swiftly, but to the dying child it seemed an age. She lay there; her life breath ebbing fast, waiting for her mother, that she may die in her arms. Angels filled the lowly cabin, and held their outstretched arms to receive the spirit of a sinless babe, as soon as it would leave the mortal clay it animated. Soon, soon would it have been borne on high, for the rattle in the child's throat had almost commenced, when a hurried footstep was heard at the door, and Mrs. Wentworth, pale and tired entered the room.

The hand of Death was stayed for awhile, for the presence of the mother started anew the arteries of life, and the blood once more rushed to the cheeks of the dying. Ella held out her arms as her mother approached her, with some medicine in her hand. As she gazed upon her child, Mrs. Wentworth started back, and uttered a faint exclamation of anguish. She saw the worst at a glance, and placing aside the medicine, she seized her child's extended hands, and bending over her, pressed her darling daughter to her heart.

"Here aunty," she said, as soon us she had released Ella, "Here is some money, run and call a physician at once."

The old negro took the money and moved off.

"Tell him to come instantly," she called out after the negro. "It is a matter of life and death, and there is no time to lose."

"Too late, too late! poor people," said the old woman, as she hurried on her mission of mercy.

It was too late. No science on earth could save Ella from death, and none on high save the Infinite Power, but He knew not of it. His eyes were still turned away from the Soldier's Wife and her children.

Mrs. Wentworth remained silent, looking at her child as she gasped for breath. Of what use was the money she had committed a crime to obtain? Of what avail were her supplications to God? It were thoughts like these that passed rapidly through her mind, as she speechlessly gazed at the fast sinking form of her child. Ella saw her agony, and tried to soothe her mother.

"Come nearer to me, mother," she said. "Come near and speak to me." Mrs. Wentworth drew near the bedside, and bent her face to the child.

"What do you wish, darling?" she asked.

"Mother, I am dying—I am going to Heaven," Ella said, speaking with an effort.

A smothered sob, was the only response she met with.

"Don't cry mother," continued the child. "I am going to a good place, and do not feel afraid to die."

Shaking off her half maddened feeling, Mrs. Wentworth replied. "Don't speak that way, darling. You are not going to die. The physician will soon be here, and he will give you some thing which will get you better."

Ella smiled faintly. "No, mother, I cannot get better; I know I am going to die. Last night, while sleeping, an angel told me in my dream, that I would sleep with God to-night."

"That was only a dream, darling," Mrs. Wentworth replied, "you will get well and live a long time."

As she spoke the old negro returned, accompanied by a physician. He was one of these old fashioned gentlemen, who never concern themselves with another's business, and therefore, he did not enquire the cause of Mrs. Wentworth, and her family being in so poor a dwelling. His business was to attend the sick, for which he expected to be paid; not that he was hard-hearted, for, to the contrary, he was a very charitable and generous man, but he expected that all persons who required his advice, should have the means of paying for the same, or go to the public hospital, where they could be attended to free of charge. His notions were on a par with those of mankind in general, so we cannot complain of him.

Approaching Ella, he took her hand and felt the pulse which was then feebly beating. A significant shake of the head, told Mrs. Wentworth that there was no hope for her child's recovery.

"Doctor," she asked, "will my daughter recover?"

"Madam," he replied, "your child is very, very ill, in fact, I fear she has not many hours to live."

"It cannot be," she said. "Do not tell me there is no hope for my child."

"I cannot deceive you, madam," he replied, "the child has been neglected too long for science to triumph over her disease. When did you first call in a medical practitioner?" he added.

"Not until you were sent for," she answered.

"Then you are much to blame, madam," he observed bluntly. "Had you sent for a physician three weeks ago, the life of your child would have been saved, but your criminal neglect to do so, has sacrificed her life."

Mrs. Wentworth did not reply to his candid remarks. She did not tell him that for weeks past her children and herself had scarcely been able to find bread to eat, much less to pay a doctor's bill. She did not tell him that she was friendless and unknown; that her husband had been taken prisoner while struggling for his country's rights; that Mr. Elder had turned herself and her children from a shelter, because she had no money to pay him for the rent of the room; nor did she tell him that the fee he had received, was obtained by theft—was the fruit of a transgression of God's commandments.

She forgot all these. The reproach of the physician had fallen like a thunderbolt from Heaven, in her bosom. Already in her heart she accused herself with being the murderess of her child. Already she imagined, because her poverty had prevented her receiving medical advice, that the accusing Angel stood ready to prefer charges against her for another and a greater crime, than any she had ever before committed.

"Dying! dying!" she uttered at last, her words issuing from her lips, as if they were mere utterances from some machine. "No hope—no hope!"

"Accept my commiseration, madam," observed the physician, placing his hat on, and preparing to depart. "Could I save your child, I would gladly do so, but there is no hope. She may live until nightfall, but even that is doubtful."

Bowing to Mrs. Wentworth, he left the room, in ignorance of the agony his reproach had caused her, and returned to his office. Dr. Mallard was the physician's name. They met again.

Ella had listened attentively to the physicians words, but not the slightest emotion was manifested by her, when he announced that she was dying. She listened calmly, and as the doctor had finished informing her mother of the hopelessness of her case, the little pale lips moved slowly, and the prayer that had been taught her when all was joy and happiness, was silently breathed by the dying child.

"Mother," she said, as soon as Dr. Mallard had left the room. "Come here and speak to me before I die."

"Ella! Ella!" exclaimed Mrs. Wentworth wildly. "Did you not hear what the physician said?"

"Yes, mother," she answered, "but I knew it before. Do not look so sad, come and speak to me, and let me tell you that I am not afraid to die."

"Ella, my darling child," continued Mrs. Wentworth in the same strain. "Did you not hear the physician say it is my neglect that had caused you to be dying?"

"I heard him mother, but he was not right," she replied.

"Come nearer," she continued in an earnest tone. "Sit on the bed and let me rest my head on your lap."

Seating herself on the bed, Mrs. Wentworth lifted the body of the dying child in her arms, and pillowed her head on her breast. The old negro was standing at the foot of the bed, looking on quietly, while the tears poured down her aged cheeks. Mrs. Wentworth's little son climbed on the bed, and gazed in wonder at the sad aspect of his mother, and the dying features of his sister.

"Mother," said the child, "I am going to Heaven, say a prayer for me." She essayed to pray, but could not, her lips moved, but utterance was denied to her.

"I cannot pray, darling," she replied, "prayer is denied to me."

The child asked no more, for she saw her mother's inability to comply with her wishes.

The little group remained in the same position until the setting sun gleamed through the window, and shed a bright ray across the bed. Not a sound was heard, save the ticking of the old fashioned clock on the mantle piece, as its hands slowly marked the fleeting minutes. The eyes of the dying child had been closed at the time, but as the sunlight shot across her face she opened them, and looked up into her mother's face.

"Open the window, granny," she said.

The old woman opened it, and as she did so, the round red glare of the sun was revealed, while the aroma of thousands wild flowers that grew beneath the window, entered the room, and floated its perfume on the autumn air.

"Mother," said the dying child.

Mrs. Wentworth looked down upon her child.

"What is it darling," she asked.

"Let brother kiss me," she requested.

Her little brother was lifted up and held over her. She pressed a soft kiss upon his lips.

"Good-bye, granny," she said, holding out her hand to the negro.

The old woman seized it, and the tears fell faster, on the bed than they had hitherto done. Her humble heart was touched at the simple, yet unfearing conduct of the child.

"Mother, kiss me," she continued. "Do not be sad," she added, observing her mother's pale and ghastly countenance. "I am going to a world where no one is sick, and no one knows want."

Stooping over her dying child, Mrs. Wentworth complied with Ella's request, and pressed her brow in a long and earnest kiss. She had not spoken a word from the time her child requested the old woman to open the window, but she had never for an instant, ceased looking on the features of her dying daughter, and she saw that the film was fast gathering on her eyes.

After her mother had kissed her, Ella remained silent for several minutes, when suddenly starting, she exclaimed: "I see them, mother! I see them! See the Angels coming for me—Heaven—mother—Angels!" A bright smile lit her features, the half-opened eyes lit up with the last fires of life; then as they faded away, her limbs relaxed, and still gazing on her mother's face, the breath left the body.

There was a rush as of wind through the window, but it was the Angels, who were bearing the child's spirit to a brighter and a better world.

CHAPTER TWENTY-FIRST.

THE INTRUSION.

As soon as the breath had left her child's body, Mrs. Wentworth removed the corpse from her lap and laid it on the bed; than standing aside of it, gazed upon all that remained of her little daughter. Not a tear, not a sigh, not a groan denoted that she felt any grief at her bereavement. Except a nervous twitching of her mouth, her features wore a cold and rigid appearance, and her eye looked dull and glassy. She spoke not a word to those around her who yet lived. Her little boy was unnoticed, no other object but the dead body appeared to meet her view.

There are moments when the fountains of grief become dried up. It was so with Mrs. Wentworth. The sight of her dead child's face—beautiful in death—for it wore a calm and placid exterior, too life-like for death, too rigid for life, awoke no emotion in her bosom; nor did the knowledge that the infant would soon be placed in the grave, and be forever hidden from the gaze she now placed on it so steadfastly, cause a single tear drop to gather in her eye, nor a sigh to burst from her pale and firmly closed lips. And yet, there raged within her breast a volcano, the violence of whose fire would soon exhaust, and leave her scarred and blasted forever. At that moment it kindled with a blaze, that scorched her heart, but she felt it not. Her whole being was transformed into a mass of ruin. She felt not the strain on the tendrils of her mind; that her overwrought brain was swaying between madness and reason. She only saw the lifeless lineaments of her child—the first pledge of her wedded affection—dead before her.

It came to her like a wild dream, a mere hallucination—an imagination of a distempered mind. She could not believe it. There, on that lowly bed, her child to die! It was something too horrible for her thoughts, and though the evidence lay before her, in all its solemn grandeur, there was something to her eye so unreal and impossible in its silent magnificence that she doubted its truthfulness.

The old negro saw her misery. She knew that the waters which run with a mild and silent surface, are often possessed of greater depth, than those which rush onward with a mighty noise.

"Come missis," she said, placing her hand on Mrs. Wentworth's shoulder. "De Lord will be done. Nebber mind. He know better what to do dan we do, and we must all be satisfy wid his works."

Mrs. Wentworth looked at the old woman for a moment, and a bitter smile swept across her countenance. What were words of consolation to her? They sounded like a mockery in her heart. She needed them not, for they brought not to life again the child whose spirit had winged its flight to eternity, but a short time since.

"Peace old woman," she replied calmly, "you know not what you say. That," she continued, pointing to the body of Ella, "that you tell me not to mourn, but to bend to the will of God. Pshaw! I mourn it not. Better for the child to die than lead a beggar's life on earth."

"Shame, shame missis," observed the old woman, very much shocked at what appeared to her the insensibility of Mrs. Wentworth. "You musn't talk dat way, it don't do any good."

"You know not what I mean, auntie," Mrs. Wentworth answered in a milder tone. "Why did I come here? Why did I bring my child ill and dying from a shelter, and carry her through the night air, until I found a home in your lonely cabin? Do you know why?" she continued with bitterness. "It was because I was a beggar, and could not pay the demands of the rich."

"Poh lady!" ejaculated the old woman. "Whar is your husband."

"My husband?" she replied. "Ah! where is he? Oh, God!" she continued wildly. "Where is he now while his child lies dead through destitution, and his wife feels the brand of the *thief* imprinted upon her forehead? Why is he not here to succor the infant boy who yet remains, and who may soon follow his sister? Oh, God! Oh, God! that he should be far away, and I be here gazing on the dead body of my child—dead through my neglect to procure her proper medical attendance; dead through the destitution of her mother."

"Nebber mind, missis," observed the old negro soothingly, "De chile is gone to heaben, whar it wont suffer any more."

"Peace!" exclaimed Mrs. Wentworth passionately. "Do not talk to me of Heaven. What has God done to aid me in my misery? Has he not suffered me to feel the pangs of hunger, to see my children deprived of bread, to permit me to stain my whole existence with a crime? The child is gone to Heaven. Aye! there her sinlessness and innocence might give her a welcome, and she may be happy, but the blank left in my heart, the darkness of my mind, the cheerless and unpropitious future that unveils itself before my aching eyes, can never be obliterated until I am laid in the grave beside her, and my spirit has winged its flight to the home where she now dwells."

She spoke slowly and earnestly, but her words were of despair not of grief. Motioning to the old woman that she desired no further conversation, Mrs. Wentworth again fixed her gaze upon the dead features of her child. On them she looked, until the tablet of her memory contained but one impress, that of her daughter's face. All records of past suffering, all anxiety for the present, all prayer for the future, were driven away, and solitary and alone the image of the dead child filled their place, and in that lone thought was concentrated all that had transpired in her life for months past. It was the last remaining bulwark to her tottering mind, and though it still held reason dominant, the foundation of sanity had been shaken to such an extent that the slightest touch and the fabric would fall from its throne and crumble to dust at the feet of madness. But this was unknown to God. He who knoweth all things still kept his eyes away from the mother and her children.

"Dead! dead!" said, Mrs. Wentworth, swaying her body to and fro. "My angel child dead! Oh, God!'" she continued, passing her hand across her brow. "That I should live to see this day, that this hour of bereavement should ever be known to me. Oh! that this should be the result of my sufferings, that this should be the only reward of my toils and prayers."

The blood rushed to her face, and her whole form trembled with an uncontrollable agitation; her bosom heaved with emotion, and the beatings of her heart were heard as plain as the click of the clock on the mantlepiece. Stooping over the dead body she clasped it in her arms, and pressed the bloodless and inanimate lips in a fond embrace. It was the promptings of a mother's heart. She had nursed the child when an infant, and had seen her grow up as beautiful as the fairies so often described by the writers of fiction. She had looked forward for the day when the child would bloom into womanhood, and be a blessing and a comfort in her old age. All these were now forever blighted. Not even the presence of her son awoke a thought within her that the living remained to claim her care and affection. He was but a link in the chain of her paternal love, and the bonds having been broken she looked on the shattered fragment and sought not to unite what yet remained in an unhurt state.

When she rose from her stooping posture her face had resumed its cold and rigid appearance. Turning to the old negro who was looking on in silent wonder and grief, she enquired in a calm tone: "Have you any of the money left that I gave you this morning?"

"Yes, missis," she replied. "I got some left."

"How much is it?" asked Mrs. Wentworth.

"Twelve dollars," she answered, counting the notes that she had taken from her pocket.

"Will that be enough to pay for a coffin for my child?" Mrs. Wentworth enquired.

"I don't know, but I spect it will do," replied the old negro.

"To make sure that it will be enough," observed Mrs. Wentworth, "here is some more money to pay for it." As she spoke she handed several notes to the old woman. "And now," she continued, "I want you to go out and order a coffin, as I want the child to be buried to-morrow morning."

"I spec I better get de parson to preach over de poor chile," remarked the old woman, who was a strict member of the church, and very superstitious in relation to the evils that would accrue from a departure from all that is laid down in religious tenets.

"Yes, yes!" Mrs. Wentworth replied. "But there is no necessity of going for him this evening, wait until early in the morning, that time will do well enough."

The old woman curtsied and moved out of the room. Arriving in town she entered an undertaker's shop and enquired if he could furnish a coffin by the next morning. On his answering in the affirmative she paid him twenty dollars, the amount charged, and hastened back to her cabin. The interest manifested by this old woman, was that usually shown to all persons in distress by the faithful slave of the South. She had not even learned Mrs. Wentworth's name, but the sight of her sad and haggard features, as well as the death of Ella, had awaken a feeling of sympathy for the unfortunate family; thus we see her obeying the orders of her accidental guests, without making any objections. But to return to the dead.

As soon as Mrs. Wentworth was left alone, her face assumed its natural appearance, and the rigid expression it had hitherto worn was dispelled. Opening a bundle she had brought front her room, she took out a white dress. It was one of the few remaining articles of clothing she possessed, and had only been saved at the earnest solicitation of the little Ella. It was her bridal robe; in that she had walked up to the altar and plighted her troth to the loved husband who was now a prisoner and far away. The first and last time she had worn it was on that day, and as she gazed on it the memory of the past rushed upon her. She thought of the hour when, as a blushing bride, she leaned on the proud form of her lover, as they walked together in the sacred edifice to register those vows that bound them in an indissoluble tie, and unite their hearts in a stronger and holier love than their lover's vows had done. Then she know not what sorrow was. No gift of futurity had disclosed to her the wretchedness and penury that after years had prepared for her. No, then all was joy and happiness. As she stood by the side of her lover her maiden face suffused with blushes, and her palpitating heart filled with mingled felicity and anxiety as she looked down on the bridal dress that covered her form. No thought, no dream, not even a fear of what after years would bring to her, stirred the fountain of fear and caused her a single pang. And now—but why trouble the reader with any further remarks of the past?

That is gone and forever. We have seen her tread the paths in which all that is dismal and wretched abides; we have seen herself and her children lead a life, the very thought of which should cause us to pray it may never be our lot. Words can avail but little. They only fill the brain with gladness for awhile to turn to horror afterwards. We have but to write of the present. In it we find misery enough, we find sorrow and wretchedness, without the hand of compassion being held forth to help the miserable from the deep and fearful gulf with which penury and want abound.

The wedding dress was soiled and crumpled; the bunches of orange blossoms with which it was adorned, lay crushed upon its folds—a fit appearance for the heart of the owner—It looked like a relic of grandeur shining in the midst of poverty, and as its once gaudy folds rested against the counterpane in the bed, the manifest difference of the two appeared striking and significant.

For a moment Mrs. Wentworth gazed upon this last momento of long past happiness, and a spasm of grief contracted her features. It passed away, however, in an instant, and she laid the dress across the dead body of her child. Drawing a chair to the bedside, she took from her pocket a spool of thread, some needles and her scissors. Selecting one of the needles, she thread it, and pinning it in the body of her dress, removed the wedding gown from the body of her child, and prepared to make a shroud of it. Rapidly she worked at her task, and before darkness had set in, the burial garment was completed, and the body of Ella was enclosed in the last robe she would wear on earth.

The body of the dead child looked beautiful. The snowy folds of the dress were looped up with the orange blossoms which Mrs. Wentworth had restored to their natural beauty. On her cold, yet lovely brow, a wreath of the same flowers was placed, while in her hand was placed a tiny ivory cross, that Ella had worn around her neck while living. The transformation was complete. The dress of the young and blooming bride had become the habiliments of the dead child, and the orange blossoms that rested on its folds and on the brow of Ella, were not more emblematical for the dead than they had been for the living.

"Oh! how pretty sister looks," exclaimed the little boy, who could not comprehend why the dead body lie so motionless and stiff. "Wake her up, mother," he continued, "she looks so pretty that I want her to stand up and see herself."

Mrs. Wentworth smiled sorrowfully at her son's remarks, but she did not remove her features from the dead. The saint-like expression of her child, and the placid and beautiful face that lay before her devoid of animation, had awoke the benumbed feelings of affection within her. A bright light flashed across her brain, and the long pent up tears, were about to flow, when the door was widely opened, and a dark shadow spread itself over the body of Ella. Checking her emotion, Mrs. Wentworth looked around and beheld the figure of Mr. Swartz, accompanied by two police officers.

She spoke not a word at first, for in an instant the cause of his visit was known. One look she gave him, which sunk into the inmost depths of his soul; then turning to the dead child, she slowly extended her hand and pointed to it.

"There," she said at last. "Look there," and her face again wore its former colorless and rigid aspect.

CHAPTER TWENTY-SECOND.

IMPRISONMENT OF THE SOLDIER'S WIFE.

We must now take a glance back at the time that Mrs. Wentworth committed her act of despair in taking the package of money from the safe. Mr. Swartz, as we stated, was then gazing intently at the open pages of his ledger, and, in her leaving the room hurriedly, did not take any other notice of her, than mere glance. He then resumed his calculations, nor did he rise from his seat for nearly three hours afterwards, so intent was he on the books before him. Rising up at last, he walked to the safe, and observing that the package of money was gone, called out to his clerk, who quickly answered the summons and entered the room.

"Vere is dat package of money I had on de safe dis morning?" he enquired, as soon as the clerk had entered.

"I have not seen anything of it, since I gave it into your hands this morning at nine o'clock," the clerk replied.

"Vell, I put it on top of dis safe," observed Mr. Swartz, "and I forgot to lock it up, ven Mr. Elder came in, and kept me talking nearly two hours, den de beggar came in and remained for a long time. After dat I vas busy mit the ledger, and didn't think of it."

"Perhaps you have placed it somewhere else, and cannot recollect where," remarked the clerk, who was apprehensive that Mr. Swartz would charge him with having stolen the money.

"No, I didn't," answered Mr. Swartz, "De monish vas put down on de top of the safe, for I remember putting it down here myself," he added, pointing to the spot where the money had been.

"You had better search about before you make certain of that," said the clerk. "See if it is not in your pocket you may have placed it there, and at the same time believe that you placed it on your safe."

"Mine Cot!" answered Mr. Swartz, "I tell you I put the package on de safe. See here," he continued, searching his pockets, and emptying them of whatever they contained. "Don't you see dat de monish is not in my pockets. It vas on de safe und unless somebody removed it, it never could have gone away."

"You should be certain, sir, before you insist that you placed it on the safe," remarked the clerk. "Look in the draw of your desk, it may have been placed there as well as any other place."

With a gesture of impatience Mr. Swartz opened the drawers of the desk, and removing everything they contained searched carefully among the large number of papers for the missing package. It was not there however, and turning to the clerk who was standing near by, he pointed to the table to indicate the fact of its absence among the papers he had taken from the drawers.

"I told you it vash not tere," he remarked. "Somebody has taken te monish, and, py Cot! I vill find out who has got it."

"Don't be so hasty in your conclusions, sir," said the clerk. "Let us search the room carefully, and see whether it has not been mislaid by you. It will never do," he added, "to charge anybody with having taken the money, when it may be lying about the room."

"Vere can it pe lying?" asked Mr. Swartz angrily. "I tell you it vash on te safe, and tere ish no use looking any where else."

"That maybe so, sir," replied the clerk, "but if you will give me permission I will search the room well before you take any further steps in the matter."

"You can look if you like," observed Mr. Swartz, "but I know tere ish no chance of your finding it, and it ish only giving yourself trouble for noting."

"Never do you mind that, sir," the clerk answered. "I am willing to take the trouble."

Removing the books from the top of the safe he carefully shook them out, but the package was not among them. He then replaced them and turned the safe round, with the hope that the money might have fallen under it. The same success, however, attended him, and he was compelled to renew his efforts. Everything in the room was removed without the package being found. After a minute and diligent search he was compelled to give up the work in despair, and ceasing he stood trembling before Mr. Swartz, who, he momentarily expected, would charge him with having committed a theft. But for this fear he would never have taken the trouble of upsetting and replacing everything in the room, but would have been perfectly satisfied for his employer to sustain the loss.

"Vell!" said Mr. Swartz. "I suppose you ish satisfied dat te monish ain't here."

"Its disappearance is very singular," replied the clerk. "If, as you say, the package was laid on the safe and never removed by you, somebody must have taken it away."

"Of course, somepody tock it," remarked Mr. Swartz. "How te tevil could it go mitout it vash taken away py somepody?"

"Do you suspect any one of having stolen it," asked the clerk, turning as white as the shirt he wore.

"Did you ever come near de safe to-day," asked Mr. Swartz, abruptly.

"Me, sir?" said the now thoroughly frightened clerk. "No, I—No sir—I—never came further than the door each time you called to me."

"I can't say dat Mr. Elder vould take it," observed Mr. Swartz, "and all I remember now dat you didn't come anyvere near de safe, I can't tink who could have taken the monish."

Assured by his manner that Mr. Swartz had dismissed all idea of charging him with the theft, the clerk's confidence returned, and he ceased stuttering and trembling.

"Do you think the woman who was here could have taken it?" he enquired, and then added: "The last time I entered this room while she was here, I remember seeing her standing near the safe, with her elbow on the top."

"By Cot!" exclaimed Mr. Swartz, striking the table with his hand. "She must be de very person. She vanted me to give her monish, and she must have seen de package lying on the safe and taken it avay."

"It is no use wasting any time then," said the clerk, "you must endeavor to find out where she stays, and have her arrested this evening."

"Vere can I find her house?" asked Mr. Swartz.

"You will have to track her," answered the clerk. "The first place you had better go to is Elkin's drug store, for I saw the woman enter there after leaving here."

Mr. Swartz made no reply, but taking up his hat he walked out of his office, and proceeded to the drug store. The druggist, who had noticed the wild and haggard appearance of Mrs. Wentworth, informed him, in reply to his enquiries, that such a person as the one he described had purchased several descriptions of medicines from him, and on leaving his store, she had walked up the street. This being the only information that the druggist could give, Mr. Swartz left the store, and after many enquiries discovered where Mrs. Wentworth resided. He immediately returned to his store, and mentioned his discovery to the clerk.

"You had better go at once and take out a warrant against her for robbery;" remarked the clerk, "and take a couple of policemen with you to arrest her."

Starting to the City Hall, Mr. Swartz took out a warrant against Mrs. Wentworth for larceny, and procuring the assistance of two policemen, he started for the old negro's cabin, determined to prosecute the thief to the utmost extent of his power and the law. Having informed our readers of his conduct on discovering that his money had been stolen, we will continue from where we left off at the close of the last chapter.

Mrs. Wentworth on perceiving Mr. Swartz and the two policemen, had pointed to the dead body of her child, and pronounced the solitary word, "there," while her face became cold and expressiveless.

Involuntarily looking in the direction pointed out by Mrs. Wentworth, the three men started with awe as their eyes fell upon the beautiful face of the dead child. One of the policemen, who was a devout Catholic crossed himself, and withdrew from the entrance of the door, but the other policeman and Mr. Swartz quickly shook off all feelings of fear that had passed over them.

"Here is de voman," said Mr. Swartz, pointing to Mrs. Wentworth. "Dis is de voman who shtole mine monish."

As he spoke she turned her face towards him, but the mute anguish of the mother did not cause a sentiment of regret to enter Mr. Swartz's heart, at the part he was acting towards her.

"Arrest her," continued Mr. Swartz, "I vant you to take her to de jail, where she can be examined, and to-morrow morning I can have her up before de Mayor."

"Not to-night," exclaimed Mrs. Wentworth in a hollow voice. "Leave me with the dead body of my child; after she is buried you can do as you please with me."

"I knows better tan to do dat," observed Mr. Swartz, "by to-morrow morning you vould be a pretty far avay from Shackson."

"I will not move from this cabin an inch further than to the burial ground," replied Mrs. Wentworth, "but if you fear it is my intention to escape, let one of your policemen remain here and watch me to night."

Mr. Swartz stepped to the threshold of the door, and consulted the two men on the possibility of complying with her request, but one refused through superstition, while the other declined in consequence of his being on the night watch.

"I can't agree to your vishes," said Mr. Swartz, as soon as the conference was over, and he returned to the bedside. "De policemen vont remain here."

"Then do you trust me," she replied. "By the holy name of God, I implore you not to tear me from the body of my child, but if that name has no weight with you, and as I perceive it is useless to appeal to you by the sacred tenets of Christianity, let me pray you, that as a man, you will not descend to such brutality as to force me from the dead body that now lies before you, and deprive me of performing the last sad rites over her. In the name of all that is humane, I plead to you, and, oh, God! let my supplications be answered."

"Dere is no use of you talking in dat vay to me," said Mr. Swartz in a coarse and brutal tone. "It vas in de same sthyle dat you vent on dis morning, ven you vas begging me, and den you afterwards shtole my monish."

As he finished speaking, the old negro entered the cabin, and perceiving the intruders, enquired the cause of their presence. The Catholic who was an Irishman, briefly explained the object of their visit to the astonished old woman, who never conceived for a moment that Mrs. Wentworth had been guilty of theft.

"De Lor!" she exclaimed, as soon as her informant had concluded his remarks. "Who would'a believe it? Poh people, dey is really bad off," and she hurried to Mrs. Wentworth's side.

Mrs. Wentworth had paid no attention to the colloquy between the old negro and the policeman; she was engaged in appealing to Mr. Swartz, not to remove her to jail that night.

"You must have some feelings of humanity within you," she was observing. "You must have some touch of pity in your heart for my condition. Do not send me to jail to-night," she continued in an earnest tone. "If your own heart is steeled against the sorrows of a helpless and wretched woman; if the sight of that dead face does not awaken a spark of manly pity within you, let me entreat you, by the memory of the mother you once had, not to tear me from the body of my child. The hours of night will pass of rapidly, and by the dawn of morning my daughter shall be buried."

This was the first touch of feeling she had manifested, and though no tears bedewed her cheeks, the swelling of her bosom and the anguished look she wore, told of sorrow more terrible than if tears had come.

The wretch was unmoved. He stood there, not thinking of the solemn and heart-rending scene before him, but of the money he had lost, and the chance of its being found on the person of Mrs. Wentworth.

"Do your duty, policemen," he said, without appearing as if he had heard her remarks.

"It is well," she said, and walking up to the bedside of her dead child, she lifted the body until it almost assumed a standing position. "Farewell child, farewell forever!" she continued, covering the lifeless face with kisses. "See this!" she said, turning to the men, "see the result of beggary and starvation.

Look upon it, you have had it in your power to save me from this desolation, and rejoice in your work. Here, take me," she added, laying down the corpse. "Take me from the presence of the dead, for if I remain gazing at it much longer, I will indeed go mad."

Walking up to the old woman, Mrs. Wentworth continued. "Auntie, I leave my child's body with you. See that it is buried and mark the spot where it rests, for oh! I feel that the day is not far distant when my weary head will rest in peace at last, when that time arrives, I desire to be buried by the remains of her who now lies there. For the little boy who is here, keep him Auntie, until his father claims him, and should his father never return, take him before some man high in position, and tell him that a wretched mother leaves him to the care of his country, as a momento of one of the patriot band who died in her service."

The old negro fell upon her knees before the speaker, and burst into tears, while even the rude policemen were touched by her remarks, Mr. Swartz alone remained unmoved, the only feeling within him was a desire that the work of confining her in jail should be completed.

"And now one last farewell," continued Mrs. Wentworth, again embracing the corpse. Another instant and she was out of the room followed by the three men, and they proceeded in the direction of the jail.

The old negro fell on her knees by the side of the bed, burying her head in the folds of the counterpane, while the tears flowed freely from her eyes. The little boy nestled by her side sobbing and calling for his mother.

"Don't cry chile," said the old negro, endeavoring to console him. "Your mammy will come back one of dese days," then recollecting the words of Mrs. Wentworth in reference to him, she took him in her arms, and continued, "poh chile, I will take care ob you until your father come for you."

Thus did the good hearted slave register her promise to take care of the child, and her action was but the result of the kind treatment she had received from her owner. She had been taken care of when a child by the father of her present owner, who was no other than Dr. Humphries, and now that she had grown old and feeble, he had provided her with a home, and supported her in return for the long life of faithful service she had spent as his slave.

The next morning at about nine o'clock, a hearse might have been seen in front of the old woman's cabin. Without any assistance the negro driver lifted a little coffin from the chairs on which it rested in the room, and conveyed it into the hearse. It then drove off slowly, followed by the old negro and the infant, and drove to the burial ground. There a short and simple prayer was breathed over the coffin, and in a few moments a mound of earth covered it. Thus was buried the little angel girl, who we have seen suffer uncomplainingly, and die with a trusting faith in her advent to Heaven. No long procession of mortals followed her body, but the Angels of God were there, and they strewed the wood with the flowers of Paradise, which though invisible, wafted a perfume into the soul sweeter than the choicest exotics of earth.

From the grave of the child we turn to the mother, to see if her sufferings died with the body of the Angel which had just been buried. They had not, for still the eye of God was turned from the Soldier's Wife, and he saw not the life of misery and degradation that she was leading.

CHAPTER TWENTY-THIRD.

THE COMMITTAL.

On the morning that Ella was buried, Mrs. Wentworth was carried before the Mayor, and charges preferred against her for robbery. The package containing the remainder of the money had been found on her person the night previous, and this evidence was brought forward against her.

"What are your charges against this woman, Mr. Swartz," began his Honor.

"Vell your Honor," replied that individual, "I vill tell dem in but few words. Dis voman called at my shtore yesterday, and begged me for monish. I gave her von tollar, but she vouldn't take it, and after she left de shtore I found out dat a package of monish, dat was on de safe was gone, I den called mine clerk, and I look for de monish, and he looked for de monish, but ve neider of us find de monish. Den I say dat certainly somepody must take dish monish, and he say so too; den ve remember dat dis voman vas leaning against de safe, and he told me of it, and I remember too, and—"

"Explain your charges against the woman as briefly as possible, Mr. Swartz," interrupted the Mayor. "I have not time to stay here listening to a long round-about story."

"Von minute your Honor, von minute," replied the wretch. "I will soon finish de account. As I vas saying, I remember dat dis voman vas standing leaning by de safe and mine clerk tells me to go to de Trug Shtore, as de voman vent in dere, and I goes in de Trug Shtore, and Mr. Elkin he tells me dat de voman did come in dere and py some physic and dat she valk up de street, and I goes up de street and—"

"For goodness sake, Mr. Swartz, let me beg of you to conclude your remarks as soon as possible and not detain the Court with unnecessary statements," again interrupted the Mayor, "I see no use for you to repeat all that you did. Just come to the point at once and I will be able to decide whether this woman is to be committed or not."

"Shust von minute longer, your Honor," Mr. Swartz answered, "I vill finish directly. Vell, you see, I vent in te street, and I goes up te street, and I asks te beoples if tey see tis voman, and von of tem say he not see te voman, and I ask anoter and he not see te voman, and I ask anoter again and he not see te voman eider."

"If you are going to continue this nonsense all day let me know, and I will prepare myself to listen, as well as to return the other prisoners to jail until to-morrow," observed His Honor. "It appears as if you can never get through your tale. Speak quickly and briefly, and do not keep me waiting."

"Shust vait a little vile more nor not so musht," replied Mr. Swartz, and continuing his story he said, "I ask everybody if tey sees dis voman and dey say dey not sees te voman, and after I ask everybody von man tell me dat he sees dis voman valk up de shtreet, and I go up de shtreet von little more vay and—"

"In the name of Heaven cease your remarks," exclaimed the Mayor, who had become thoroughly exasperated at the narrative of Mr. Swartz.

"Gootness," observed that gentleman, "did you not shay I vas for to tell vy I pring dis voman up?"

"Yea," replied His Honor, "but I did not expect you to give me a long narrative of all that occurred during the time while you were looking for where she lived."

"Veil, I vill soon finish," he remarked, "as I was saying, I goes up de shtreet von little more vays and I ask anoder man vere dis voman vas, and he shust look on me and shay he vould not tell noting to von tam Tutchman, and I go to von oder man and he show me von little log cabin, and I goes up dere softly and I sees dis voman in dere."

"All this has nothing to do with the charge you have preferred against her," the Mayor said, "let me know upon what grounds you prefer the charge of robbery against her."

"Vell, ven I sees her I valks pack to mine Shtore and I talks mit mine clerk, and he say I vas have to take out a varrant, and I comes to de City Hall and I takes out de varrant, and I takes two policemen and I goes to te cabin and finds dis voman dere, and she peg me not to take her to jail, but I vouldn't pe pegged and I pring her to jail."

"Mr. Swartz, if you don't conclude your remarks at once I will be necessitated to postpone your case until to-morrow; I I am tired of hearing your remarks, every one of which has been to no purpose. You say the package of money that you lost was found on this woman, and that she had been in your store the same day and had leaned against the safe on the top of which the money had been placed by you."

"Dat's shust it," replied Mr. Swartz. "Ven I go mit te voman to te jail te jail man search her and find te monish in her pocket, and it vas te same monish as I had stolen off te safe.—But te monish vas not all dere; over tirty tollars vas taken out of it, and dat vas vat dis voman sphent, and I—"

"That's enough, Mr. Swartz," interrupted the Mayor. "You have said enough on the subject, and I will now proceed with the accused."

While Mr. Swartz was speaking Mrs. Wentworth remained as silent as if she had not heard a word he said. Her appearance was calm, nor was there anything remarkable about her except a strange unnatural brightness of the eye.

"Well, my woman," continued the Mayor, "what have you to say in extenuation of the charge."

"Nothing, Sir," she replied, "I have nothing to say in defense of myself. The money was found on my person, and would alone prove me guilty of the theft. Besides which, I have neither desire nor intention to deny having taken the money."

"What induced you to steal?" asked the Mayor.

"A greater tempter than I had ever met before," she replied. "It was necessity that prompted me to take that money."

"And you sphent tirty-tree tollers of it, py gootness," exclaimed Mr. Swartz, in an excited tone.

"As you acknowledge the theft," said the Mayor, "I am compelled to commit you to prison until the meeting of the Superior Court, which will be in four days from this."

Mrs. Wentworth was then committed back to prison, and Mr. Swartz returned to his store.

The spirit of the child had reached God and at that moment was pointing to her mother below. The day of rest is near.

CHAPTER TWENTY-FOURTH.

RETURN OF ALFRED WENTWORTH—A STRANGER.

After long weeks of pain and illness Alfred Wentworth became well enough to return to the Confederacy. He was accordingly sent down by the first flag of truce that went to Vicksburg after his recovery, and two days after the committal of his wife arrived at Jackson, where he was warmly welcomed by Harry.

"I am delighted to see you, my dear friend," he exclaimed, shaking his hands warmly, "you have no idea the suspense I have been in since my escape, to learn whether you were re-captured. It would have reproached me to the last hour of my life had you been killed by those cursed Yankees."

"I came pretty near it," replied Alfred, smiling at his friend's earnestness.

"You were not hurt, were you?" enquired his friend.

"The slight matter of a few minie balls, lodged in different parts of my body, is all the injury I received," he answered.

"I suppose that occasioned your not coming with the first lot of prisoners," Harry remarked.

"Yes," he replied, "when the cartel was arranged and orders were given for the prisoners to prepare for their departure from Camp Douglas, I was still suffering from my wound, and the doctors declared me unable to move for several days. An excited mind soon brought on fever, which so prostrated me that the days extended to weeks before I was able to leave the hospital."

"I am heartily glad to see you once more safe on Confederate soil, at any rate," observed Harry, and he added, "as I will insist upon your staying at my house while you are here, let me know where your baggage is, that I may hate it removed."

"I am staying at the Burman House, but what little baggage I possess is at Vicksburg."

"Then take a walk with me to the residence of Dr. Humphries," said Harry, "and I will introduce you to my betrothed."

"I thank you," Alfred replied, "but the present state of my wardrobe does not admit of my appearing before ladies."

"Pshaw," observed Harry, "that is the least part of the question. Let me know what you desire and I will get it for you directly."

"I have about seven hundred dollars in Confederate money with me," answered Alfred, "if you will show me some store where I can purchase a decent suit of clothes; that will be all I shall trouble you for."

"Take a walk with me to Lemby's clothing store and you will find a fine outfit there."

Drawing Alfred's arm in his, Harry conducted him to Lemby's clothing store, where a suit of clothing was bought. They then proceeded to the Bowman House and entered Alfred's room.

"My furlough is only for thirty days," Alfred remarked, while engaged in dressing himself, "and how I am to send in a letter to New Orleans and receive an answer before that time expires I cannot conjecture."

"What do you wish to write to New Orleans for," asked Harry.

"Why, to wife," answered Alfred, "I think it is about time that she should hear from me."

"My dear friend," replied Harry, "your wife is not in New Orleans, she is in the Confederate lines."

"Where is she?" he enquired, eagerly.

"I could not tell you that," Harry answered, "but of one thing you may be certain, she is not in New Orleans."

"How do you know that?" he asked.

"Dr. Humphries purchased a negro girl the day before I returned; she gave her name as Elsy, and said she was belonging to Mr. Alfred Wentworth, of New Orleans. On being questioned why she had left the city, the girl said that her mistress with your two children had been forced to leave by Beast Butler, who would not allow her to go also, but that, being determined to follow your wife, she had ran the blockade and came into the Confederate lines.".

"And did my wife sell her to anybody else?" enquired Alfred.

"Wait a moment, my dear friend, and I will tell you," answered Harry. "The girl did not see her mistress at all, for she was arrested on her arrival in this city, and having no papers, as well as no owner, she was sold according to law, and was purchased by Dr. Humphries, at whose residence she is now. I would have told you this when we first met, but it slipped my memory completely."

"But where could my wife have gone to?" remarked Alfred. "I do not know of any person in the Confedcrate lines with whom she is acquainted, and where she can get the means to support herself and children I have not the least idea."

"That she has been to Jackson I am certain," Harry replied, "for no sooner did I hear what the girl had informed Dr. Humphries, than I endeavored to find out where she resided. I searched the register of both the hotels in this city and found that she had been staying at this hotel; but the clerk did not recollect anything about her, and could not tell me where she went to on her departure from this city. I also advertised in several newspapers for her, but receiving no information, was compelled to give up my search in despair."

"I thank you for your remembrance of me," observed Alfred. "This intelligence, however, will compel me to apply for an extension of my furlough, so that I may be enabled to find out where my wife and children are. I am very much alarmed at the news you have given me."

"I hope your wife and children are comfortably situated, wherever they may be; and could I have discovered their residence, I should have made it my duty to see that they wanted for nothing."

"I know it, I know it," said Alfred, pressing his friend's hand, and he continued, "you will favor me on our arriving at Dr. Humphries' by obtaining an interview for me with Elsy; I desire to know the cause of my wife's ejectment from New Orleans."

"As soon as you are ready let me know and we will start for the Doctor's," Harry answered, "where you will find the girl. Dr. Humphries told me that he intended returning her to you or your wife as soon as he discovered either of you. So in the event of your finding out where Mrs. Wentworth lives, she will be promptly given up."

"No, no," Alfred remarked, hurriedly, "the Doctor has purchased her and I do not desire the girl unless I can return the money he paid for her. If you are ready to go," he added, "let us leave at once."

The two friends left the hotel and soon arrived at the residence of Dr. Humphries. The Doctor was not at home, but Emma received them. After introducing Alfred to her, and engaging in a brief conversation, Harry requested her to call Elsy, as he desired her to speak with his friend. The fair girl complied with his request by ringing the bell that lay on the table; her call was answered by the slave in person.

On entering the room Elsy made a low curtsey to the gentlemen, and looked at Alfred earnestly for a moment, but the soldier had become so sunburnt and altered in features that she failed to recognize him.

"Do you not remember me, Elsy?" enquired Alfred, as soon as he perceived her.

His voice was still the same, and running up to him, the girl seized his hand with joy.

"I tought I knowed you, sah," she exclaimed, "but you is so change I didn't remember you."

"I am indeed changed, Elsy," he replied; "I have been sick for a long time. And now that I am once more in the Confederacy, it is to find my wife and children driven from their homes, while God only knows if they are not wandering all over the South, homeless and friendless. Tell me Elsy," he continued, "tell me what caused my wife to be turned out of the city?"

In compliance with his request, the girl briefly told him of the villainy of Awtry, and the infamous manner in which he had acted towards Mrs. Wentworth. She then went on to relate that, failing to achieve his purpose, Awtry had succeeded in having her expelled from New Orleans.

"Did your mistress—I beg pardon—I meant, did my wife tell you where she was going to?" enquired Alfred.

"She told me to come to Jackson, after I told her I would be sure to get away from de city," answered the girl; "but de police ketch me up before I could look for her; and since I been belonging to Dr. Humphries I has look for her ebery whar, but I can't find out whar she am gone to."

"That is enough," observed Alfred, "you can go now, Elsy, if I should want to see you again I will send for you."

"I trust you may succeed in finding your wife, sir," Emma said as the girl left the parlor.

"I sincerely hope so myself, Miss Humphries," he answered, "but Heaven only knows where I am to look for her. It will take me a much longer time than I can spare to travel over the Confederacy; in fact, I doubt whether I can get an extension of my furlough, so that I may have about three months of time to search for her."

"It is singular that she should have told Elsy to come here to her, and not to be in the city," observed Emily.

"I am afraid that my wife has, through prudence, gone into the country to live; for, with the means I left her, she could not possibly have afforded to reside in any part of the Confederacy where prices rule so high as they do here. It is this belief that makes my prospect of finding her very dim. Harry says he advertised for her in several newspapers, but that he received no information from any source respecting where she lived. I am certain she would have seen the advertisement had she been residing in any of our cities."

"She may not have noticed the advertising column of the newspaper," put in Harry, "if ever she did chance to have a copy of one that contained my notice to her. Ladies, as a general thing, never interest themselves with advertisements."

"You are right," Alfred replied, "but it is singular that some person who knew her did not see it and inform her; she surely must have made some acquaintances since she arrived in our lines, and I am certain that there are none who do not sympathize with the unfortunate refugees who have been driven into exile by our fiendish enemy."

"I am sorry to say that refugees are not as favorably thought of as they deserve," Emma remarked. "To the shame of the citizens of our Confederacy, instead of receiving them as sufferers in a common cause, they are looked upon as intruders. There are some exceptions, as in all cases, but I fear they are very few."

"Your statement will only increase my anxiety to find my wife," answered Alfred; "for if the people act as unpatriotically as you represent, there is no telling if my unfortunate family are not reduced to dire necessity, although it is with surprise that I hear your remarks on the conduct of our people. I had thought that they would lose no opportunity to manifest their sympathy with those who are now exiles from their homes, and that idea had made me feel satisfied in my mind that my wife and children would, at least, be able to find shelter."

"I do not think anyone would refuse to aid your family, my dear friend," Harry observed, "although I agree with Miss Emma, that our people do not pay as much attention to refugees as they should; but the unfortunate exile will always find a sympathizing heart among our people. You may rest assured that, wherever your wife may be, she has a home which, if not as comfortable as the one she was driven from, is at least home enough to keep herself and her children from want."

Harry Shackleford judged others by the promptings of his own heart, and as he uttered these words of comfort to his friend, he little dreamed that Mrs. Wentworth was then the inmate of a prison, awaiting her trial for robbery, and that the crime had her committed through the very necessity he had so confidently asserted could never exist in the country.

"Will you take a walk to the hotel," enquired Alfred, after a few minutes of silence, "I desire to settle my bill with the clerk."

"Certainly," he replied, rising from his chair, "I desire to conduct you to my home."

"Good evening to you Miss Humphries," said Alfred, as he walked to the door with his friend.

She extended her hand to him as she replied, "Good evening, sir—allow me to repeat my wishes for your success in finding your wife and children."

Bowing to her in reply, he left the room, accompanied by Harry.

"Do you know, Harry," he observed, as they walked towards the Bowman House, "I have a strange presentiment that all is not well with my family."

"Pshaw," replied his friend, "you are as superstitious as any old woman of eighty. Why in the name of wonder will you continue to look upon the dark side of the picture? It is more likely that your family are now comfortably, if not happily situated. Depend upon it, my dear friend, the world is not so cold and uncharitable as to refuse a shelter, or a meal to the unfortunate."

Alfred made no reply, and they walked on in silence until the hotel was reached. On entering the sitting room of the Bowman House, the two gentlemen were attracted by the loud talking of a group of men standing in the centre of the room.

"There stands an Englishman who lately run the blockade on a visit to the Confederacy," observed Harry as they approached the group; "let me introduce him to you."

Walking up to where the Englishman was, Harry touched him lightly on the shoulder.

"How are you Lieutenant Shackleford," he said, as he turned and recognized Harry.

"Very well, Mr. Ellington," answered Harry, and then added, "allow me to introduce my friend Mr. Wentworth to you—Mr. Wentworth, Mr. Ellington."

As the name of Wentworth escaped Harry's lips the Englishman started and changed color, but quickly resuming his composure, he extended his hand to Alfred.

"I am happy to make your acquaintance, sir," he observed, and then continued, "your features resemble those of a gentleman I have not seen for years—so much, indeed, that I could not repress a start as my eyes fell upon your countenance."

"I was rather surprised at seeing you start," observed Harry, "for I knew that you were not acquainted with my friend Mr. Wentworth. He was a prisoner at Camp Douglas—the prison you have read so much about—when you arrived in this country, and has only returned to the Confederacy within the last few days."

"A mere resemblance to one whose intercourse with me was not fraught with many pleasant recollections," remarked Mr. Ellington. "Indeed your friend is so much like him, both in form and features, that I really imagined that he was my old enemy standing before me!"

"A singular resemblance," said Alfred, "and one which I am rejoiced to know only exists in form and features. And now," he continued, "allow me to ask you a question."

Mr. Ellington bowed an assent.

"Were you ever in this country before?" asked Alfred.

"Yes," replied Mr. Ellington, "I visited America a few years ago, but why do you ask?"

"Because your features are familiar to me," he answered, and then enquired, "Were you ever in New Orleans."

"No, sir—no," replied Mr. Ellington, coloring as he spoke, "I was always afraid of the climate."

"The reason of my asking you," observed Alfred, "is because you resemble a gentleman with whom I was only very slightly acquainted, but who, like the party you mistook me for, has done me an injury which neither time nor explanation can repair, but," he added, "now I recollect you cannot be the party to whom I refer, for he was a Northern man, while you are an Englishman."

Before the Englishman could reply, a gentleman at the further end of the room called him by name, and, bowing to the two friends, he apologized for leaving them so abruptly, and walked off to where the call came from.

As soon as he left them Alfred went up to the clerk's office and paid his bill. The two friends then left the hotel and proceeded to Harry's residence.

"Do you know, Harry," observed Alfred, as they walked along, "I have an idea that Mr. Ellington is no Englishman, but that he is Awtry, the scoundrel who caused my wife and children to be driven from New Orleans?"

"Why do you imagine such a thing?" asked Harry.

"Only because his features are very much like those of Awtry; and the start he gave when you pronounced my name half confirms my suspicion."

"I feel certain you are mistaken," Harry remarked. "He arrived at Charleston in a blockade runner a short time ago, and brought letters of introduction to many prominent men in the South from some of the first characters in England."

"That may be," Alfred answered, "still I shall keep my eye on him, and cultivate his acquaintance. If I am mistaken it will make no difference, for he shall never know my suspicions; but if I am right in my surmise he shall answer me for his treatment of my wife and children."

"That you can do," said Harry, "but be cautious how you charge him with being a Yankee spy, and have certain proof of his identity before you intimate your suspicions to him." As he spoke they reached their destination and the two friends entered the house.

Horace Awtry, for the Englishman was none other than he, under an assumed name, had ventured to enter the Confederate lines as a spy for Sherman, who was then getting up his expedition against Vicksburg. He would have left Jackson immediately after the meeting with Alfred, but upon enquiry he learned that Mrs. Wentworth's place of residence was unknown, and his services being needed near Vicksburg decided him to remain.

CHAPTER TWENTY-FIFTH

THE TWO SLAVES—THE GLIMMER OF LIGHT.

From the time of Mrs. Wentworth's arrest and imprisonment, the old negro had paid every attention to the little boy left under her care. Knowing that she would be likely to receive punishment for having a white child living with her, she had made several efforts to see her master, but each time she called, both the Doctor and Emma were absent. She was thus compelled to wait until some opportunity offered to turn the little boy over to her master, who she knew would promptly give him a home while he remained unclaimed by his lawful guardians. In her visits to Dr. Humphries' house the old negro had met Elsy, and being pleased with the appearance of the girl, had contracted quite a friendship for her, and on every opportunity would hold a conversation with her. Having called several times without seeing her master or Emma, Elsy enquired if she had anything of consequence to impart to the Doctor, as, if she had, she would inform him on his return home.

"Yes, gal," replied the old woman, "I got a leetle boy at my cabin dat was lef dar by him mammy, and I want de boss to take him away and put him in a better place den my room."

"What chile is it, Auntie?" enquired Elsy.

"I do' know what de name is," answered the old woman, "but a lady cum to my cabin one night wid a berry sick gal chile and de leetle boy, and next day de gal die, and in de ebening some police come and take away de lady because 'she 'teal money,' and dey lef de dead chile and de libing one wid me."

"Goodness sakes, Auntie," interrupted Elsy, "what did you do wid de dead chile?"

"Why, gal, I bury her next mornin," replied the old woman, "and de leetle boy bin stayin wid me eber since; but I don't want to keep him, for dis nigger hab no right to hab white chile a keepin to herself."

"You better see de Doctor, den," Elsy observed. "When he come in I will tell him dat you want to see him patickler."

"Dat's a good gal," answered the old negro, "you tell him dat I want to see him, but don't tell him what I want him for—I rader tell him dat mysef."

"Berry well, Auntie," she replied, "de Doctor will come in about dinner time, and as soon as he is done eatin I will talk to him about it. But do you tink he will bring de chile home, yah, and take care ob him?"

"Ob course he will," said the old woman, "he neber see any body want but he get him plenty and take care ob him."

"What kind a chile is de one you had at your cabin?" asked Elsy.

"Jes de lubliest baby you eber seed in your life," answered the old negro. "He is one ob de best children I eber had taking care ob."

"Don't he cry none for his mudder," enquired Elsy.

"Ob course he cry plenty de first day," she replied, "but aterwards he behabe well, for I promise him dat he mammy will come back soon. He am a rale good chile, and I would lub to keep him wid me all time, but I 'fraid de police will get ater me for habin him."

"Dat's so," remarked Elsy, "but you can take care ob him a'ter you tell de boss—you can come here and stay."

"No, gal," she answered, "I can't leab me old cabin; I been libbing dar dese twelve years, and I got so used to it dat I can't sleep out ob it."

"Den I will take care ob de chile for you," said Elsy, "and you can come ebery now and den and see him."

"Dat's so," she, replied. "But tell me, gal," she continued, "whar you come from?"

"I come from New Orleans, Auntie," replied Elsy.

"What bring you to Jackson?" continued the old woman.

Elsy repeated the tale she had told Dr. Humphries and Alfred, and after she had concluded, the old woman clasped her hands as she exclaimed, "Sake alibe! what become ob your mistis and de childen?"

"I don't know, Auntie, but my New Orleans mass'r is here now, and I's been looking for dem."

"Why de lady and childen dat come to my cabin was from New Orleans too," observed the old negro.

"You say you don't know de name?" remarked Elsy.

"No, I forget," she answered; "but what name did your mistis hab?"

"Dey was name Wentworth," she replied.

"Wantworth—Wentworth," repeated the old woman. "No, dat don't sound like de name ob de lady, but may be I forget. What was de leetle gal name?" she added.

"Ella," replied Elsy.

"Dat's it," exclaimed the old negro, "dat's de berry name!"

"Den it was my mistis and her childen," answered Elsy, "and you say de police take her to prison for stealin."

"Yes, gal," she answered, "dey take her away from de dead body ob her chile and take her to prison for stealin."

"It ain't true," said Elsy, "my mistis is a born lady, and she wouldn't steal for anyting. I don't beliebe a word ob it."

"I don't beliebe neider," replied the old woman, "but for all dat, dey did carry her to prison because dey say she steal money."

"My poh mistis," remarked Elsy, bursting into tears, "I knowed dat some bad ting would happen to her—and I was in town so long and neber eben sawed her."

"Poh lady," observed the old negro, "she look bery bad and sorrowful like, aldough she didn't cry when de chile die; but she tan up by de bedside and look 'pon de dead face widout sayin' a word—it made me feel bad to see her."

"I must tell my master," said Elsy, "so dat he can go and take her out ob prison. It am a shame dat a lady like dat should be locked up in a prison, and Mr. Wentworth will soon take her out."

"You better not say anyting to your master about it, yet," observed the old woman. "See de Doctor and tell him; he will know what to do, and den he can tell de gemman all about it a'terwards."

"But you certain it am my mistis?" said Elsy.

"I ain't quite sure ob dat," she answered, "for de name sound different to de one I heard, and dats de reason I don't want you to say noting 'bout it till de Doctor enquire into de matter and find out. I must go now, gal," she added, "don't forget to tell de Doctor all 'bout it when he come home."

"I won't," replied Elsy.

The old woman then left the house and returned to her cabin, where she found the little boy amusing himself on the floor with some marbles.

Dr. Humphries, accompanied by Harry, returned home at the usual hour. After dinner Elsy requested him to speak to her for a few minutes—a request which he promptly complied with.

"Well, my good, girl, what do you wish with me?" he enquired.

"Oh! sir," she replied, "I hab found out whar my mistis is."

"You have," answered Dr. Humphries, rather astonished at the intelligence, "where is she?" he added.

"In prison, sah," she replied.

"In prison!" exclaimed the Doctor, "for what?"

"I don'no, sah," she replied, "but I hear it is for stealing."

"Who gave you the information?" asked Dr. Humphries.

"It was your ole slave what libs in de cabin, up town," answered Elsy.

"And how did she learn anything about Mrs. Wentworth?" enquired Dr. Humphries.

"My Mistis went dere wid her chil'en, sah, and her little daughter died in de ole woman's cabin."

"Good God!" exclaimed the Doctor, "and how was it that I have heard nothing about it until now?"

"It only was a few days ago," replied Elsy, "and Auntie come here ebery day, but you and Miss Emma was not at home ebery time, and she only tole me about it dis mornin."

"Are you certain that the woman who has been carried to jail is your Mistress?" asked Dr. Humphries.

"No sah," she answered, "Auntie say dat de name am different, but dat de name ob de leetle gal am de same."

"And the little boy you say has been under the care of the old woman ever since," remarked Dr. Humphries.

"Yes sah," Elsy replied, "but she want you to take him away from her, so dat he may be under a white pusson, and das de reason why she been here wantin' to see you bout it."

"Very well," said. Dr. Humphries, "I will attend to it this evening; in the meantime do you remain here and go with me to the cabin and see if the child is your Mistress'."

Elsy curtsied as she enquired, "Shall I tell my Master 'bout dis, sah?"

"No, no," replied the Doctor, "he must know nothing about it until I have arranged everything for his wife and removed her from prison. Be certain," he continued, walking to the door, "that you do not breathe a word about this until I have seen your Mistress and learned the reason of her imprisonment."

On returning to the parlor, where Harry and Emma were seated, Dr. Humphries called him aside and related what he had heard from Elsy. The young man listened attentively, and was very much shocked to hear of Mrs. Wentworth's being imprisoned for theft. He knew that Alfred was the soul of honor, and he could not conceive that the wife of his friend would be guilty of such an offense.

"It is impossible to believe such a thing," he said, after Dr. Humphries had concluded, "I cannot believe that the wife of such a man as Alfred Wentworth would commit an offense of such a nature; it must be some one else, and not Mrs. Wentworth."

"That we can find out this evening," observed the Doctor. "Let us first call at the cabin of my old slave and find out whether the child in her keeping is one of Mrs. Wentworth's children."

"How will we be able to discover," asked Harry. "It appears by your account that the boy is a mere infant, and he could hardly be expected to give an account of himself or his parents."

"I have removed any difficulty of that nature," replied Dr. Humphries, "Elsy will accompany us to the cabin, and she will easily recognize the child if he is the son of your friend."

"You are right," Harry remarked; and then continued, "I trust he may not be, for Alfred would almost go crazy at the knowledge that his wife was the inmate of a prison on the charge of robbery."

"I hope so myself, for the sake of your friend," said Doctor Humphries, "Mr. Wentworth appears to be quite a gentleman, and I should greatly regret his finding his wife in such an unfortunate position as the woman in prison is represented to be."

"I know the spirit of the man," remarked Harry, "he is sensitive to dishonor, no matter in what form or shape it may come, and the knowledge that his wife was charged with robbery would be a fearful blow to his pride, stern and unyielding as it is."

"If it is his wife, and she has committed a theft, I pity her, indeed; for I am sure if she is the lady her husband represents, nothing but the most dire necessity could have induced her to descend to crime."

"Ah, sir," replied Harry, "Heaven only knows if it is not through want. Alfred Wentworth feared that his wife was living in penury, for he knew that she was without adequate means. If she has unfortunately been allowed to suffer, and her children to want with her, what gratification is it for him to know that he was proving his loyalty to the South in a foreign prison while his wife and children were wanting bread to eat in our very midst?"

"It will indeed be a sad commentary on our patriotism," remarked Dr. Humphries. "God only knows how willing I should have been to serve the poor woman and her children had they applied to me for assistance."

"And I fervently wish that every heart in the State beat with the same feeling of benevolence that yours does," replied Harry. "However, this is no time to lament or regret what is inexorable; we must see the child, and afterwards the mother, for, no matter whether they are the family of Alfred Wentworth or not, the fact of their being the wife and child of a soldier entitles them to our assistance, and it is a debt we should always willingly pay to those who are defending our country."

"You are right, Harry, you are right," observed the Doctor, "and it is a debt that we will pay, if no one else does it. Do you return to Emma, now," he continued, "while I order the buggy to take us to the cabin."

Leaving Harry, Dr. Humphries went to the stable and ordered the groom to put the horse in the buggy. He was very much moved at the idea of a friendless woman being necessitated to steal for the purpose of feeding her children, and in his heart he sincerely wished she would not prove to be the wife of Alfred Wentworth. Harry's story of his friend's chivalrous conduct to him at Fort Donelson, as well as the high toned character evinced by Alfred during the few days acquaintance he had with him, had combined to procure a favorable opinion of the soldier by Dr. Humphries; at the same time, he could not conceive how any one could be so friendless in a land famed for the generous hospitalities of its people, as the South is; but he knew not, or rather he had never observed, that there were times when the eye of benevolence and the hand of charity were strangers to the unfortunate.

There are no people on the face of the earth so justly famed for their charitable actions as that of the Confederate States.—Before the unfortunate war for separation commenced, every stranger who visited their shores was received with a cordial welcome. The exile who had been driven from his home on account of the tyranny of the rulers of his native land, always found a shelter and protection from the warm hearts and liberal hands of the people of this sunny land; and though often times those who have received the aid and comfort of the South, shared its hospitalities, received protection from their enemies, and been esteemed as brothers, have turned like vipers and stung their generous host, still it passed it heedlessly and was ever ready to do as much in the future as it had done in the past. As genial as their native clime, as generous as mortals could ever be, those who sought the assistance of the people of the South would find them ready to accord to the deserving, all that they desired. It was indeed a glorious land; blooming with the loveliest blossoms of charity, flowing with the tears of pity for the unfortunate, and resplendent with all the attributes of mortal's noblest impulses. Gazing on the past, we find in the days of which we write no similitude with the days of the war. A greater curse than had fallen on them when war was waged on their soil, had fallen on the people of the South; all those chivalrous ideas which had given to her people a confidence of superiority over the North had vanished from the minds of those who had not entered the Army. It was in the "tented field" that could be found those qualities which make man the true nobility of the world. It is true that among those who remained aloof from active participation in the bloody contest were many men whose hearts beat with as magnanimous a pulsation as could be found in those of the patriots and braves of the battle-field; but they were only flowers in a garden of nature, filled with poisonous weeds that had twined themselves over the land and lifted up their heads above the purer plants, which, inhaling the tainted odor emitted by them, sickened and died, or if by chance they remained and bloomed in the midst of contamination, and eventually rose above until they soared over their poisonous companions, their members were too few to make an Eden of a desert, and they were compelled to see the blossoms of humanity perish before them unrewarded and uncared for, surfeited in the nauseous and loathsome exhalations of a cold and heartless world, without the hand of succor being extended or the pitying tear of earth's inhabitants being shed upon their untimely graves.

While they, the curse of the world, how was it with them? But one thought, one desire, filled their hearts; one object, one intention, was their aim. What of the speculator and extortioner of the South, Christian as well as Jew, Turk as well as Infidel! From the hour that the spirit of avarice swept through the hearts of the people, the South became a vast garden of corruption, in which the pure and uncorrupted were as pearls among rocks. From the hour that their fearful work after gain commenced, charity fled weeping from the midst of the people, and the demons of avarice strode triumphant over the land, heedless of the cries of the poverty stricken, regardless of the moanings of hungry children, blind to the sufferings it had occasioned and indifferent to the woe and desolation it had brought on the poor.

But all this was seen by God, and the voice of Eternity uttered a curse which will yet have effect. Even now as we write, the voice of approaching peace can be heard in the distance, for the waters on which our bark of State has been tossing for three years begins to grow calmer, while the haven of independence looms up before us, and as each mariner directs his gaze on the shore of liberty the mist which obscured it becomes dispelled, until the blessed resumption of happiness and prosperity once more presents itself, like a gleam of sunshine on a dark and cheerless road of life.

The eye of God is at last turned upon a suffering people. The past years of bloody warfare were not His work; He had no agency in stirring up the baser passions of mankind and imbuing the hands of men in each others blood, nor did He knowingly permit the poor to die of want and privation. He saw not all these, for the Eye which "seeth all things" was turned from the scene of our desolation, and fiends triumphed where Eternity was not, Hell reigned supreme where Heaven ruled not—Earth was but a plaything in the hands of Destiny. Philanthropy may deny it—Christianity will declare it heresy—man will challenge its truth, but it is no less true than is the universe a fact beyond doubt, and beyond the comprehension of mortals to discover its secrets.

CHAPTER TWENTY-SIXTH.

THE RECOGNITION.

As soon as the groom had prepared the buggy, he announced to Dr. Humphries that it was in readiness. Calling Harry, who was again seated by the side of his betrothed, indulging in secret conversation, the Doctor went into the street where the buggy was.

"I will drive myself this morning, John," he remarked to the groom, "Mr. Harry will go with me."

"Berry well, sah," replied the groom, moving off.

Stepping into the buggy, followed by Harry, the Doctor took the reins in his hands and was about to drive off.

"Wait a moment," observed Harry, "has Elsy gone to the cabin?"

"No, I forgot all about her," answered the Doctor, "and I am glad you reminded me."

"You had better send for her at once, and give her orders to proceed immediately to the cabin," said Harry, "for without her we would be unable to know whether the child is that of Alfred Wentworth or of some other unfortunate soldier."

"Here, John!" called out Dr. Humphries after the retreating form of the groom, "come here to me."

The boy turned back and returned to the side of the buggy.

"Tell Elsy to come here at once," said the Doctor.

The boy moved off to comply with his master's order, and in a few moments returned, accompanied by Elsy.

"Do you go to the old woman's cabin," said Dr. Humphries, as soon as she had reached the side of the buggy, "and wait there until I arrive. There is no necessity to mention what I am going there for."

"Yes sah," replied Elsy, as she turned away to do her master's bidding.

"And now," remarked the Doctor, "we will go on and find out who these people are. But before we go, I had better purchase a few things that will relieve the necessities of the child."

With these words the Doctor drove off, and on arriving in front of a store, drew in the reins and, alighting, shortly after returned with several packages, which he placed in the buggy and, re-entering it, he drove to the cabin of the old slave. On arriving there the Doctor and Harry found the old woman and the child seated in the room talking. The boy appeared quite contented, now that his grief at the loss of his sister and departure of his mother had subsided, and was laughing merrily when they entered. He was dressed very cleanly and neatly by the old slave, who had expended all her savings in purchasing suitable cloths for him, and his appearance excited the remark of the Doctor and his companion the moment they entered the threshold of the room and saw him.

"Good day sah," said the old negro, rising and curtseying as soon as the two gentlemen entered.

"God day, Auntie," said the doctor, "how are you getting on."

"Berry well," answered the old woman, and then added, "I'm mighty glad you come here dis day, for I want to talk wid you 'bout dis here chile."

"I have heard all about him, Auntie," said the Doctor, "and have come here expressly for the purpose of learning something about his parents."

"'Spose dat gal Elsy tell you," observed the old woman, snappishly, nettled because she had not the opportunity of telling her master the tale of Mrs. Wentworth and her children.

"Yes, Auntie," he replied, "Elsy told me, but not before I had asked her all about those unfortunate people, so you must not be mad with her."

"She might ha' waited till you see me befo' she say anyting about it," remarked the old woman.

"Never mind that, Auntie," replied the Doctor, who knew the old woman's jealous disposition and wanted to pacify her. "Has Elsy been here yet?"

"No sah," she replied, "I aint seen her since mornin'."

"She will be here directly, then," he remarked, and seating himself the Doctor waited the arrival of Elsy.

"Come here my little man," said Harry, who had been sitting on the bed during the dialogue between the old slave and her master.

The child walked up to him and placed his arms on Harry's knees.

"What is your name," enquired the young man, lifting the child up on his knees.

"My name is Alf," he replied.

"Alf what?" asked Harry.

The child looked at him enquiringly, not understanding the question.

"What is your mother's name," continued Harry, perceiving that the boy was unable to answer his question.

"My ma's name is Eva," he answered.

"And your sister's?" asked Harry.

"My sister is named Ella," replied the child, and then added, mournfully, "but she is gone from here; they took her out in a little box and put her in the ground, and Granny says she is gone to heaven; and my ma," he continued, "some bad men carried away, but Granny says she will soon come back—wont she?" and his innocent face looked up confidingly in Harry's.

"Yes, my boy," he answered, "your ma will soon come back to you."

"There appears no doubt of the identity of this family," remarked Harry to Dr. Humphries, after a short pause, "everything we have yet discovered indicates that Alfred Wentworth's wife and children have passed a fearful life since their expulsion from New Orleans."

"Poor woman and children," observed the Doctor, dashing away a tear, "could I have known their penury, I should have been only glad to relieve them, and even now, it is not too late for us to benefit this child and his mother. As soon as Elsy arrives here I shall remove the boy to my house and visit the mother in jail."

"I do not think it advisable to move the child until you have succeeded in obtaining the release of Mrs. Wentworth," answered Harry. "His father may chance to see him, and, under the circumstances, would discover where his wife was; which discovery I desire to avoid as long as possible. The best thing that you can do is to leave the boy here for twenty-four hours longer, by which time bail can be procured for his mother, and I shall endeavor to silence the charge, so that there may be no necessity for a trial."

"May not Mr. Wentworth see the child and recognise him before we have accomplished his mother's release," enquired the Doctor.

"I do not think it likely," he replied, "Alfred will not visit so remote a vicinity, and the child need not be carried into the business portion of the city."

"I shall leave him here, then, as you think it advisable," remarked the Doctor; "it cannot injure him to remain in this cabin for a day longer, while it might lead to unpleasant discoveries should he be removed."

Harry and the old gentleman remained silent for some time, when Elsy entered the room. No sooner did the girl see the boy than she recognized her master's child, and taking him in her arms caressed him with all the exhibitions of affection the negro is capable of.

"Dis am Mas Alfred own chile" she exclaimed to Harry and the old gentleman, "and who would thought dat him would be libin' here."

"I supposed it was your master's child, my good girl," observed the Doctor, and then added, as he rose from his seat, "you can stay here with him until dark, when you had better return home; meanwhile, I do not wish you to let Mr. Wentworth know that his wife and child are in this city, nor do I wish you to take him out of this cabin. Come Harry," he continued, "let us go now and see the mother; she will be able to give us full details of her unfortunate life and to inform us of the cause for which she is in prison."

Leaving the cabin, the two gentlemen re-entered the buggy and drove to the Mayor's office. Finding him absent, they proceeded to his residence, and, after briefly narrating the tale of Mrs. Wentworth and her family, requested permission to visit her.

"Certainly, my dear sirs," replied Mr. Manship, such being the name of the Mayor, "take a seat while I write you an order of admittance."

In a few minutes the order to admit Dr. Humphries and his companion in the female's ward of the prison was written. Returning thanks to the Mayor, the two gentlemen started for the prison, and on showing the permit, were ushered into the cell occupied by Mrs. Wentworth.

"Good God!" exclaimed Harry, as he looked upon the squalid and haggard form of the broken hearted woman, "this surely cannot be the wife of Alfred Wentworth."

Mrs. Wentworth had paid no attention to the visitors when they first entered, but on hearing her husband's name pronounced, rose from her crouching position and confronted the speaker. The name of the one she loved had awoke the slumbering faculties of the woman, and, like a flash of electricity on a rod of steel, her waning reason flared up for a moment.

"You spoke my husband's name," she said in a hoarse tone, "what of him?"

"He is my friend, madam," replied Harry, "and as such I have called to see you, so that you may be removed from this place."

"Thank you," she answered; "yours is the first voice of charity I have listened to since I left New Orleans. But it is too late; I have nothing now to live for.

Adversity has visited me until nothing but disgrace and degradation is left of a woman who was once looked upon as a lady."

"There is no necessity for despondency, my good madam," observed Dr. Humphries. "The misfortunes which have attended you are such as all who were thrown in your situation are subject to. Our object in coming here," he continued, "is to learn the true cause of your being in this wretched place. Disguise nothing, but speak truthfully, for there are times when crimes in some become necessity in others."

"My tale is briefly told," she answered. "Forced by the cruelty of a villain to leave my comfortable home in New Orleans, I sought refuge in the Confederate lines. I anticipated that refugees would meet with a welcome from the more fortunate people of the South. In that I was disappointed; for when my means gave out, and every endeavor to procure work to feed my children had failed—when I had not a dollar to purchase bread for my innocent babes, I applied for assistance. None but the most dire necessity would have prompted me to such a step, and, Oh, God! when it was refused—when the paltry pittance I asked for was refused, the hope which I had clung so despairingly to, vanished, and I felt myself indeed a miserable woman. Piece after piece of furniture went, until all was gone—my clothing was next sold to purchase bread. The miserable life I led, the hours spent with my children around me crying for bread—the agonizing pangs which rent my mother's heart when I felt I could not comply with their demand— all—all combined to make me an object of abject misery. But why describe my sufferings? The balance of my tale is short. I was forced out of the shelter I occupied because I could not pay the owner his rent. My oldest child was then ill, and in the bleak night wind, canopied by heaven alone, I was thrust, homeless, from a shelter owned by a man whose wealth should have made him pause ere he performed such an act. With my sick child in my arms I wandered, I knew not where, until I found she had fainted. Hurrying to a small cabin on the road, I entered and there discovered an old negro woman. From the lips of a slave I first heard words of kindness, and for the first time aid was extended to me. Applying restoratives, my child revived and I waited until next morning, when I returned once more to ask for aid. A paltry sum was handed to me, more for the sake of getting rid of the mendicant than to relieve my distress. I felt that the sum offered was insufficient to supply the demands of my sick daughter and my starving boy. I was turning in despair away when my eye lit upon a package of money resting on the safe. For a moment I hesitated, but the thought of my children rose uppermost in my mind, and, seizing the package I hurried from the store."

"So you did take the money," said Harry.

"Yes," she replied, "but it did me little good, for when the doctor was called he pronounced my daughter beyond medical skill. She died that evening, and all the use to which the money was appropriated, was the purchase of a coffin."

"Then the—the—" said Harry, hesitating to use the word theft, "then, it was not discovered that you had taken the money until your child was dead and buried."

"No," she said, "listen—my child lay enrobed in her garment of death, and the sun was fast declining in the west, when Mr. Swartz and two constables entered the room and arrested me. On my bended knees I appealed to him not to tear me from the body of my child. Yes," she continued, excitedly, "I prayed to him in the most abject manner to leave me until my child was buried. My prayers were unavailing, and from the window of this cell I witnessed a lonely hearse pass by, followed by none other than my infant boy and the kind old negro. Oh God! Oh God!" she went on, bursting into tears and throwing herself on the wretched pallet in the cell, "my cup of misery was then full, and I had drained it to the very dregs. I have nothing more to live for now, and the few days longer I have to spend on earth can be passed as well in a prison as in a mansion."

"Not so," interrupted Dr. Humphries, "I trust you will live many, many years longer, to be a guardian to your child and a comfort to your husband."

"It cannot be," she answered sadly. "The brain, overwrought, will soon give way to madness, and then a welcome death will spare me the life of a maniac. I do not speak idly," she continued, observing the look they cast upon her; "from the depths of my mind, a voice whispers that my troubles on earth will soon be o'er. I have one desire, however, and should like to see it granted."

"Let me know what that is," remarked Dr. Humphries, "and if it lies in my power it shall be accorded to you with pleasure."

"Your companion spoke of my husband as his friend; does he know where he is at present, and if so, can I not see him?"

"I promise that you shall see your husband before many days. Until you are removed from this place I do not think it advisable, but," continued Harry, "I shall, on leaving this place, endeavor to secure your release."

Mrs. Wentworth made no answer, and, speaking a few words of consolation and hope to her, the two gentlemen left the prison. The next morning Harry called on the Mayor and asked if Mrs. Wentworth could be bailed, but on his honor mentioning that her trial would come off the next day, the court having met that evening, he determined to await the trial, confident that she would be acquitted when the facts of the case were made known to the jury. On the same day he met Alfred Wentworth, who informed him that he was more strongly impressed than ever in the belief that the pretended Englishman was a spy.

"I will inform you of a plan that will prove whether you are right or not," observed Harry, when he had concluded. "Tomorrow at about three o'clock in the evening persuade him to visit the Court House. I will be present, and if he is really the spy you imagine, will have full evidence against him."

"What evidence?" enquired Alfred.

"Never do you mind," he replied, "just bring him and there will be plenty of evidence found to convict him if he is a spy. By the way," he continued, "you said you suspected him to be the same man who caused your wife to be turned out of New Orleans?"

"Yes," Alfred answered, "but why do you ask?"

"Oh, nothing in particular," he replied, "only in the event his being Awtry, you will have a double motive in finding out whether he is a spy or not."

"You are right," observed Alfred, "but whether he is Awtry or not, I should deem it my duty to the Government to ferret out the true status of that man, and to have him brought to justice if he is really a spy. Your request to carry him to the Court House is a strange one, and I will cheerfully comply with it, although I cannot see how his being there will enable us to make the discovery."

"Leave that to me," answered Harry, "and content yourself with believing that I am certain it will prove whether he is an Englishman or a Yankee."

With that the two friends departed and Harry returned home much perplexed at the manner he had arranged for the husband and wife to meet.

CHAPTER TWENTY-SEVENTH.

TRIAL OF MRS. WENTWORTH—THE ADVOCATE.

The morning for the trial of Mrs. Wentworth arrived, and at the hour of ten she appeared in the court. Her appearance was changed since we last saw her. The kind hearted daughter of Dr. Humphries had visited her the day before with a supply of clothing, and though her features retained their haggard and care-worn expression, none who looked upon her as she entered the court room could have failed to perceive that she was a lady and unlike a majority of females brought before a jury to answer grave charges. Her case did not excite any notice until she appeared, when the pinched and sharp face presented to the spectators, and the evidence her lady-like demeanor gave of her being a different subject from that usually presented, awoke a feeling of interest in the crowd, and many enquiries were made of the nature of the charge made against her. None, however, could inform the inquisitors, and they awaited the reading of the charges.

As Mrs. Wentworth entered the room she cast a look at the jury box, and a shudder came over her as she perceived Mr. Elder sitting among the jurymen. She knew that he would not favor the dismissal of the case; but a gleam of hope presented itself in the person of Dr. Mallard, who she believed to be a good man, notwithstanding his abrupt and true remarks at the bedside of her dying child. These were the only two persons present she knew, save and except Mr. Swartz, who stood near by, ready to give his evidence against her. But from him she expected nothing; nor did she intend to ask one word of favor or mercy. There was no disposition within her to sue for mercy, nor did she purpose denying or palliating her having taken the money.

After the usual delay, Mrs. Wentworth was placed in the prisoners' stand and the charges preferred against her. In his usual style Mr. Swartz proceeded to narrate his business connection with the accused, and stated that he had done everything he possibly could for her, but that, not satisfied with receiving his bounty, she had stolen his money. His story was given in a conclusive and plausible manner, and on his clerk certifying to what his employer had said, the chances for the accused appeared very dim. What added more to the evidence against her, was the conduct of Mr. Elder, who, rising from his seat briefly stated that, from his intercourse with her, he believed Mrs. Wentworth to be an unprincipled and dishonest woman.

"On what ground do you make that assertion, Mr. Elder?" enquired the Judge.

"As I stated before, in my intercourse with her," he replied.

"And may I ask of what nature your intercourse was?" asked the Judge.

"It would delay the court were I to state what business transactions have taken place between this woman and myself," answered Mr. Elder. "When I arose, it was simply to state my belief in her dishonesty."

"You should have appeared on the witness' box, if you desired to give evidence against the accused," remarked the Judge. "As it stands, your assertions cannot be taken as evidence against her. If you desire to appear as a witness for the accuser, say so, and I will then be prepared to hear what you may have to say."

"I have no such desire," replied Mr. Elder, seating himself.

"And now my good woman," said the Judge, turning to Mrs. Wentworth, who had remained a silent listener to all that had been said against her, "let me know what you may have to say against the charges brought against you. By your appearance and general demeanor you have seen better days, and it is a source of regret that I should see any one bearing evidence of once living in a different sphere from the one you now occupy, brought before me on a charge of robbery. Let me now know what you have to say on this charge."

"I can say nothing," she replied.

"Well, then, do you plead guilty, or not guilty?" asked the Judge.

"Not Guilty!" thundered Harry, in an excited manner. He had been unavoidably delayed from accompanying Mrs. Wentworth to the Court House, and had just arrived. "Not guilty! I repeat, and, as counsel for the accused, I beg leave to make a few remarks."

"Certainly, Lieutenant Shackleford," answered the Judge, who knew Harry well.

The remarks of Harry, and his excited manner, awoke the waning interest in the case, and the crowd clustered closer round the railings.

"Your honor, and gentlemen of the Jury," began Harry, as soon as he had become calm enough to speak: "It is now nearly two years since I appeared in a civil capacity before a court of justice, and I had thought that while this war lasted my services would have been solely on the battle-fields of my country, and not in the halls where law is dispensed. But the case which I have appeared to defend, is so unlike those you ordinarily have before your honorable body, that I have, for a while, thrown off the armor of the soldier, and once more appear as the lawyer. You will pardon my apparent digression from the subject at issue, but as I see many looks of surprise at my seemingly strange conduct, I deem it but justice to myself that I should explain my motive for so acting.

"It is now nearly two years ago that a soldier in a happy and comfortable home in New Orleans bade adieu to a fond wife and two promising children. As the tear-drop trickled down the cheek of his lovely and blooming wife, he whispered a word of comfort and solace to her, and bade her be cheerful, for the dark cloud which covered the political horizon of his country would soon be dispelled by the bright sunshine of liberty. But the tear that fell on her cheek was not of regret; for she felt that in leaving her he obeyed the call of his country, and was but performing a duty he owed to his native South. The tear was brushed away, and she smiled in his face at the glowing words of hope and comfort he spoke to her. They were full of promise, and as each syllable fell on her ear, they awoke an echo in her heart, until the love of the wife paled before the enthusiastic patriotism of the Southern woman, and the dangers of the battle-field became hidden before the vision of the honor and glory which awaited the patriot hero. Then she bade him adieu with a smile, and they departed, full of love and hope.—Oh! gentlemen, let me take a glance back at the home and household war had then severed. Before our treacherous enemy had proclaimed war against us, this soldier's home was a model of earthly joy and felicity. It is true, there was no wealth to be found there, but there was a bright and more glorious gift than wealth can command; there was happiness, and this, combined with the love borne by this soldier for his wife, served to make them pass their years of wedded life in comfortable union. Years pass over their heads, and two children are sent to bless them, and they were cherished as priceless gifts. When the call to arms resounded through the South, this husband, like thousands of others, ceased his civil pursuits, and enlisted under the banner of his country. None but the purest and loftiest motives of patriotism, and a sense of duty, prompted him to the step; and though he knew that in so doing he would leave his wife deprived of her natural protector, and subject to privations, he thought, and with every right, that those who remained at home would shield a soldier's wife from danger, and he trusted on the means at his disposal to keep her from penury and destitution. After making preparation for his wife and children, he bade them adieu, as I have described already, and departed for Virginia, whose soil had already been invaded by the vandals of the North.

"And now, gentlemen, lest you should think by my intimating that this soldier was not wealthy, I meant he was also poor in society, I will state that he and his wife held as high a position in the social circle of New Orleans as the most favored of fortune. His wife, this unfortunate lady, who now stands before you charged with theft, is the daughter of one who was once wealthy, but on whom adversity fell shortly before her marriage. Think not that the haggard and care-worn features before you were always such. There was a time, not long distant, when the bloom of youth and beauty could be seen in that sunken cheek and that sharpened face; but adversity has reduced one of

God's fairest works to the wretched and unfortunate condition she is now in. Pardon my digression, for the tale I have to tell cannot be briefly recited; it is necessary that I shall speak in full, and though I may tire you by my lengthy remarks, you must hear them with patience, for they are necessary in this defence, and are equally needed to hold up to the scorn and contempt of every patriotic spirit in the land, two men who have disgraced their sex and entailed misery, aye, and degradation, on an unfortunate woman."

"If his honor, the judge, will permit me," interrupted Mr. Elder, "I should like to decline serving as a juryman on this case."

"Silence!" exclaimed Harry, before the judge could reply. "You are already sworn in, and I desire that you shall remain where you are."

"I cannot possibly excuse you, Mr. Elder," remarked the judge, in a tone of surprise, "the case has progressed too far already for any excuse. Continue, Lieutenant Shackleford," he continued, speaking to Harry.

"As I was observing," Harry went on, "this soldier departed for Virginia, and shortly after his departure, a villain, who had addressed his wife in former years and been rejected, assumed the sheep's garb and resumed his acquaintance with her. Many were the kindnesses he extended towards her, and the delicate manner in which he performed those little acts of courtesy, that lend a charm to society, disarmed any suspicion of his sincerity of purpose. But under the guise of friendship, the villain designed to overcome a lonely woman. With that subtlety and deception which every *roue* possesses, he ingratiated himself in her confidence and favor until she began to regard him in the light of a brother. But the hour approached when the mask he had worn so long would be thrown aside and his unhallowed desires be avowed. The soldier was taken prisoner at Fort Donelson, and within four months after, New Orleans fell. Then the persecutions of the unprincipled villain commenced. A Northern man, he did not at the commencement of the war avow his sympathies to be with the people of his section, but, pretending friendship for the South, remained in our midst until Butler and his infamous cohorts had gained possession of the city, when he proclaimed himself a Unionist, and gaining the favor of that disgrace to the name of man, was soon able to intimidate the cowardly or beggar the brave. One of his first attempts was to compel this lady to yield to his hellish passions. With contempt she spurned his offers and ordered him never more to cross the threshold of her house. Swearing vengeance against her, he left, and on the following morning she received an order to leave the limits of the city, that day, and prepare to enter the Confederate lines. The dangers which then threatened her, she deemed vanished, for she feared more to remain in the midst of our enemies than to enter our lines. The order was therefore received with joy, and she prepared to depart. Though a pang of sorrow may have filled her heart at being compelled to relinquish her comfortable home, though she saw before her days, weeks, months, perhaps years of hardship, not one feeling of remorse at having rejected the offers of a libertine, ever entered the mind of the soldier's wife. The time at length arrived for her to depart, and with her two children, a few articles of clothing, and a small sum of money, she was placed within our lines, far from any human habitation, and left to find a shelter as best she could.

"To this city she bent her footsteps, and here she anticipated finding an asylum for herself and children. Gentlemen, we all well know that, unfortunately for our cause and country, the evils Speculation and Extortion, had spread their leprous wings and covered our land with destitution. To a man of this city, who, before the world's eye, appeared the Christian and the man of benevolence, but who in his dealings with his fellow-men, was as vile an extortioner as the most heartless; to this man she went and hired a room in which to find a shelter. Finding she was a refugee and fearing an evil day, he bound her down by law to suffer ejectment the moment she could no longer pay the rent. Ignorant of the weapon she placed in his hands, she signed the deed, and after paying a portion of the rent in advance, left him and assumed possession. Mark well, gentlemen, what I have said. In his action we find no Christianity—no benevolence; nothing but the spirit of the extortioner is here manifested. There is no feeling of sorrow shown at her unfortunate position, no disposition evinced to shield the helpless mother and her babes. No! we find his actions narrowed down to the sordidness of the miser, the avariciousness of the extortioner. A feeling of surprise at such conduct may flit across your bosoms, gentlemen, and you may perchance doubt that I can show a man of this city, so bereft of charity, so utterly oblivious to all the better feelings of humanity, but I shall before long call his name, and give such evidence of the truth of my assertions, as will be beyond contradiction or doubt.

"To another man the soldier's wife went for the purpose of purchasing a few articles of furniture. Of him I have little to say at present. It is true that without caring who and what she was, his merchandize was sold to her at the *speculator's* price. But he had the right to charge whatever he pleased, and therefore I have nothing to say against him for that.

"Weeks passed on, and the soldier's wife found herself without the means of purchasing food for her children. The hour had at last arrived when she was utterly destitute. In the meantime her husband lay in a foreign prison, ignorant of the unhappy fate his wife was undergoing. Many are the nights we have walked to and fro on the grounds of Camp Douglas, and often has he spoken to me of his absent wife and children. I know him, gentlemen, and never in the breast of man beat a heart truer than his, nor in the minds of God's mortals were there ever finer and nobler impulses. While he was thus suffering confinement for his country's sake, his wife and children were here—in our very midst, *starving!* Aye, starving! Think of it, gentlemen—that in the midst of those who were supposed to be friends—the wife and children of a patriot were allowed to starve. Great God! is there on earth a spectacle so fearful to behold as *starvation?* And is it not enough to evoke the wrath of the Infinite, when men, surrounded by all that wealth can afford, refuse to aid and succor their starving fellow creatures?

"You may think that no man can be found who would refuse, but I tell you, gentlemen, that that man who now stands before you, was appealed to by this lady, the accused, after she had disposed of every piece of furniture in the room, save and except the bed on which her children slept. The appeal was rejected, and, despairing of help, she offered and sold to him the last remaining article of furniture. Here now is the picture. He could not lend or give her a paltry pittance; and why, forsooth? Because the money would not yield him a profit, and there was a chance of his losing it. But the moment she offered to dispose of the bed, he purchased it, for in it did the profit of the speculator lie hidden, and on it could he get his money doubled. Think not, gentlemen, that the tale you have listened to from him is the true one. It is a varnished and highly colored evidence, beneath which a wide extent of corruption can be seen, the moment its curtain is removed.

"The pittance thus obtained serves but a short time, and they are again reduced to want. The eldest child—a lovely daughter, is taken ill, and while lying on a heap of rags in a corner of the room, the man calls and demands his rent. The poor woman has no money to satisfy his demands and he orders her to leave. She appeals to him, points to her ill child; but her prayers are unavailing—and in the hour of night she is thrust from the room, homeless, penniless, friendless! Yes! he—that man who now sits in the jury-box—he— Mr. Elder, the so-called *Christian* and man of CHARITY—he, ejected this helpless woman from the shelter and forced her to wander in the night air with her sick child—her starving babes. He—the *extortioner*"—continued Harry, with every feature expressing the utmost scorn, "turned her from the wretched home she had found here, and left her to die on the sidewalks, like the veriest beggar. No touch of pity for the child, no feeling of sorrow for the innocent angel, no thought of the patriot lingering in prison, ever entered the mind of the extortioner. There was nothing but *self* then, nothing but the promptings of his own avarice, which could view with indifference the miseries of others, so long as they should redound to his own benefit and aggrandizement. I tell you that man dare not deny a word I utter. He knows that every one is true, and if my language could wither him with shame, could make him the detestation of the world, I would speak yet stronger, for pity to him is but contempt for those he has injured.

"Thus thrust out of home and shelter, the helpless mother conveyed her fainting child to a negro's cabin and there revived it. The next morning she once more called upon her accuser and petitioned him for help. He again refused to aid her, although informed that the money was intended to procure medical aid for her sick child, until at last, wearied of her importunities, he handed her the pitiful sum of *one dollar!* This was not sufficient for the purpose she desired, and she was about turning away in despair when her eye lit on a package of notes lying on the safe. Remember, gentlemen, what I have told you. She was penniless and friendless. Her child was ill and she had no means to procure medical aid. Her appeal for charity had been rejected, and can we blame her if she yielded to the tempter and took the money lying before her? We cannot. Look not on the act, gaze only on the provocation. If in hearts there dwells a shade of pity, an acme of sympathy, you cannot return a verdict of guilty. She is not guilty of theft! I unhesitatingly assert, that if to act as she has, and under the circumstances she acted, be theft, then such a thief would I become to-morrow; and in my own conscience, of the opinions of the world and confident in the forgiveness of an Almighty Father, would I commit such a theft as she has— just such an offence. I pleaded 'not guilty,' and it may surprise you that in the face of such a plea, I should acknowledge that she took the money. Again I repeat my plea. She is not guilty of theft, and to you who have hearts to you who sympathize with the sufferings of a soldier's wife—to you, whose wives and children may to-morrow be placed in a similar position—to you, I leave a verdict. But one word yet ere I am done.

"The money which she took, to what use was, it placed? To purchase a *coffin* for her child! To place the lifeless body of her daughter in its last home ere it is covered by the dust—this, and this only, was the good which accrued from it. And, gentlemen, he—Mr. Elder—is the MURDERER of that child. As such I charge him, and as such I brand him to be. But for his brutality—but for his avarice and selfish lust for gain, the mouldering corpse might now have been a blooming and happy child. And yet another word. When the so-called theft was discovered, and the accuser sought the accused, he found her by the bedside on which the dead child lay clothed in its last earthly garments. Disregarding her entreaties, she was torn from the corpse, thrust into prison, and the humble and servile hands of the negro were left to perform those sad rites which affection is ever the first to do. This is my tale, and—"

Here the excitement grew intense, and a strong feeling of indignation was manifested by the soldiers present against Mr. Swartz and Mr. Elder, and many threats were made to hang them.

CHAPTER TWENTY-EIGHTH.

THE VERDICT—THE HUSBAND AND WIFE—ARREST OF AWTRY.

It was some time before the police could restore order and quiet the excitement. At length complete silence was restored, and Harry continued:

"Such," he continued, "is the tale of this unfortunate woman, and the position in which she found herself placed should excite, a feeling of sympathy, and not induce you to punish her for an act which may be deplored but cannot be condemned. That she took the money is undeniable, but why did she take it? I have told you it was to save her child's life, and though that class of philosophers and ultra moralists who believe that there are no causes sufficient to justify her act, may declare her guilty of theft, let the promptings of your own hearts decide whether her position did not excuse, if it does not render her conduct undeserving of condemnation by a jury. But in claiming from you a verdict in favor of my client, I must take occasion to say, that your acquittal will not restore this lady to that position she formerly occupied, or remove from her mind the impress left there by an act which necessity, and necessity alone, caused her to perform. It will not restore to her the innocent child now lying mouldering in the grave, it will not reunite the broken links of affection, it will not ease the agony of the soldier when he discovers that his wife was the inmate of a prison, nor will it replace on its former firm base the mind of this unfortunate lady, which, like the pillars of some ancient edifice, totters beneath a weight of agonizing thought, soon, alas! I fear, to fall, a mass of ruin, in the vortex of insanity. The patriot soldier must return to find his daughter dead, his wife a maniac, and his only remaining child a dependent on the bounty of strangers. But one thing remains; he must turn from the spectacle thus presented and return to the battle-field a heart-broken and unhappy man. The spirit with which he formerly contended for the liberty of his country will have vanished and fled, for the remembrance of his family's fate must ever remain uppermost in his mind, and the reflections they will produce must leave a blighting scar, which no future kindness can remove, sympathy eradicate, or consolation destroy. I am done. On your good judgment and the strength of my assertions, which can be proven, if necessary, I rely for the acquittal of this lady."

As he concluded, the building shook with applause from the crowd, and Mr. Swartz and Mr. Elder trembled for their safety. Harry felt that the acquittal of Mrs. Wentworth was now secure, for the jury itself, sharing the popular feeling, gave expressions of approbation in many remarks. If the language of Harry had been simple, it had carried conviction to every soul, and all present, as they looked upon the accused, felt that her offense was fully atoned for by the chain of harrowing circumstances with which she had been bound.

And for her—the soldier's wife? She had remained a passive spectator of all that occurred. When the voice of her defender first broke on her ear, she turned and looked at him for a moment, then, as if indifferent whether his defense was successful or not, she turned her head away and listlessly gazed at the crowd. She cared not now for freedom and acquittal; she felt that the chords of reason were on the point of breaking, and but one thought, one desire, filled her mind, before they broke and madness held sway over her. It was to see that loved form, to gaze once more on those loved features, to be clasped once again in her HUSBAND'S arms. This was the sole thought, the only desire. All "fond records," all recollection of past years, all hope for future happiness, were obliterated, and nothing remained before her mind's eye but the soldier who had parted from her in New Orleans. Even the memory of her dead and of her living child had vanished, and if they were for a while brought to her mind, it was only in connection with the single desire which kept the chains of sanity united. The lineaments of every soldier in the crowd were closely and eagerly scanned, but there were none there who bore the slightest resemblance to him for whom she yearned. But still she peered into the assemblage, regardless of the efforts being made in her behalf, and it was not until the interruption narrated in the last chapter took place, that she manifested any interest in the proceedings of the court, and then it was merely by a gesture of surprise at the uproar. When Harry concluded and sat down, she again evinced astonishment, but not a syllable escaped from her lips.

After a few minutes the shouts of the crowd subsided, and at the request of the judge, silence was restored. His honor then addressed the jury.

"Gentlemen of the jury," he began, "the case before your notice has become, from one of apparent insignificance, one of intense interest and importance. A merchant of this city, well known to you all, both by his wealth and his long residence in your midst, appears before this court and accuses a woman of theft. She is arrested and every evidence of her guilt is found on her person; she does not deny the act, and is accordingly brought before you to be tried and sentenced, or acquitted, as you may, in your good judgment think best." "Overwhelming evidence is brought against her to-day, and no doubt of her having committed the theft exists. There appears little more for you to do than to find her guilty, and for me to pass the sentence. But before doing these, it is necessary that the accused shall have a defense. She is questioned, but informs the court she has nothing to say. At this stage of the proceedings, a gentleman well known to you as a rising lawyer of this place before the war commenced, and better known since then as a gallant and meritorious officer, appears as her defendant. You have heard his defense. The act of taking the money is not denied, but in his defense he claims that it was committed through dire necessity. It is true that a defense of this nature is a somewhat extraordinary one, and is new in the annals of criminal law. Still he has given you a tale of hardships and privations which he claims occurred in this city, and which, coming from any other source, may well be doubted. It is left for you to decide whether his claim for an acquittal shall be granted or not. In my remarks I do not intend to bias you one way or the other. What my opinions are will be given after your decision is announced. To you I look for that decision."

"If your honor will permit me," said Dr. Mallard, rising, "I will make a few remarks before the jury retires. The tale told by Lieut. Shackleford is correct so far as I know of it. I was called upon to attend on the sick girl mentioned in the defense, and found her in an old cabin, almost at the point of death. At the time it did not strike me as singular that a white family should be found living in such a hovel, but the tale I have just heard narrated has made me reproach myself for my blindness in not discovering that the unfortunate family were of greater respectability than can be found in the residents of log cabins. Impressed, therefore, with a firm belief in the truthfulness of the tale I have heard, I shall act accordingly."

With these remarks he resumed his seat, and in a few minutes the jury retired to decide on their verdict. Mr. Elder followed reluctantly, but had made up his mind to give consent to anything the majority should decide on. He was already apprehensive for his personal safety and was anxious to be at home again.

After a short absence the jury returned and announced they had decided on a verdict.

"What is that verdict, gentlemen?" inquired the judge. "Do you find this lady guilty or not guilty?"

"Taking all the circumstances into consideration," replied the foreman, "we find the prisoner NOT GUILTY of the charge."

For a moment the building shook to the very foundation, from the prolonged cheers of the spectators. It was not rejoicing at the escape from punishment of the guilty, that they applauded, but it was through heartfelt exultation at the acquittal of an unfortunate woman. It was the spontaneous outburst of Southern hearts, bleeding with sympathy for the oppressed and poverty-stricken soldier's wife, and swelling with indignation at the brutal and unfeeling conduct of Mr. Elder and Mr. Swartz.

Harry's eye moistened as he heard the shouts of applause, and a feeling of grateful emotion swept over him. He felt no gratification at his success in gaining her acquittal which did not spring from the loftiest and most disinterested motives. He rejoiced on account of Mrs. Wentworth and her child and the gallant soldier he had so proudly called his friend. He rejoiced to know that the fair fame of the soldier's wife stood untarnished, and that he could restore her to the arms of her husband, not as the inmate of a penitentiary, but as the acquitted accused, who had committed the act she was accused of, but was still considered by all who had heard of the case, free from crime, and pure and unstained as before the blighting handy of penury and suffering were stretched across her sorrow-beaten path.

"Madam," said the judge, when the cheering had ceased, "you have heard the verdict of the jury, acquitting you of the charge made against you by Mr. Swartz, although in your defense, it is acknowledged you did take the money, and the jury is cognizant of the fact. While your acquittal, in face of the evidence given, and your own acknowledgment as well as the acknowledgment of your counsel, may be somewhat deviating from the letter of the law, it is nevertheless in strict accordance with its spirit, and with pleasure I inform you that being acquitted you are no longer held a prisoner, but are free to go where you will. But before you leave, let me make a few remarks on this case, which in my judgment are called for by the circumstances, and which may appear again, in consequence of many parties being similarly situated. Although the jury has acquitted you, such acquittal must not be considered a license for others to go and do likewise. Where your case is one of necessity, another of a like nature may be caused through dishonesty. Your act is not applauded by thinking minds, nor did the jury intend to convey the impression that in acquitting you they considered you had performed a very meritorious act. To the contrary, they deplore the performance of a deed which cannot be thought of but with regret; at the same time they took into consideration the deplorable position into which you were placed, and declare you innocent of *theft*.

"Before closing my remarks," he continued, "I would call the attention of those present, as well as the people in general, to this case. Like this unfortunate lady, many refugees are sojourning in our midst. They should be received with welcome by those who are fortunate enough to live in peace and quiet in their happy homes. But such, I fear, is not always the case. Many respectable families who had been accustomed to all that wealth could afford, are now living, if not in absolute necessity, in very poor circumstances, and could have their position materially improved if the people of this State would offer them that assistance they need. It is not an act of charity to lend a helping hand to the refugee. We are bound together by a sympathy formed on the battle-field by the gallant men of every State now struggling side by side for our independence, and it is a matter of duty that the wives and children of the soldier shall not suffer during his absence. It is a sordid spirit that refuses to aid a helpless woman because she happens to be a refugee. This Confederacy is a home for all its sons and daughters, and when they abandon their native State, and, fleeing from a brutal enemy, come into our midst for safety and protection, we should welcome them as suffering patriots and cherish, them as they deserve. It is a hard struggle for a woman to abandon a home, surrounded by all the luxuries of life and in which happiness reigns dominant, to incur hardships and privations. In doing so her patriotism is severely tested, and nothing but the most exalted devotion to our country triumphs over her fears.

"There is yet another subject I will speak on. The two men who have figured so conspicuously in this case as the cause of this lady's sufferings, cannot be allowed to pass unnoticed. Mr. Elder is a well known gentleman of this city and has hitherto borne an irreproachable character. Did he not stand silent when accused of inhuman conduct towards this lady, I should hesitate to believe him guilty of such an atrocity. But as his silence is indicative of guilt, the horrible nature of his act comes before us with great force, and we shudder to think that any one wearing the form of humanity could so far debase the mind as to turn a helpless woman and dying child from a shelter because she had not the means of paying her debt. In so doing, Mr. Elder has displayed the spirit of the extortioner, and must feel all the stings of conscience which haunt the mind of a murderer, should his heart be not too much hardened already. He has acted a worse part than a murderer, for the assassin kills his victim through revenge, or at the worst, for pay. Here, Mr. Elder—a possessor of wealth and not needing the money—turns a tenant from his roof because she is penniless. I say nothing against him for doing so, for it was an indisputable right of his, but when we view the brutality of the act—when we think of the hardness of the heart that could not commiserate with the situation of Mrs. Wentworth—that was deaf to the appeals of a mother—blind to the illness of her child—the soul sickens with horror at the knowledge that a mortal so debased—so utterly devoid of the instincts of humanity which govern a brute—should exist on the earth. But the mask of religion is now torn from his face, and we see his own lineaments. Henceforth the scorn of all generous, minds will he receive, and turned from the respectable position he once held, must reflect on the inevitable exposure of the hypocrite some day, sooner or later. I shall leave him to the scorn and indignation of all good men. From them he will receive that punishment which his brutality, caused from his extorting spirit, deserves.

"And for Mr. Swartz, the accuser of this lady, I can see but little in extenuation of his conduct. If his business is even illegitimate, there are so many speculators in the South that it should not cause surprise that his refusal to aid this woman necessitated her taking his money. The speculator cannot be expected to have a heart tender enough to perform a charitable act. The man who will speculate on the necessities of the people, is not likely to feed the hungry. It is too true that many good men have been drawn into the vortex of speculation, but these are few in number and are isolated cases.

"Mr. Swartz has been among us long enough to imbibe the spirit and sentiments of our people, but from his action towards this lady, he does not seem to have profited by their example. A foreigner by birth, he has cast a stigma on his nation, for, with all their faults, I do not believe there is a more charitable people than the German. I have found it so, in many years of familiar intercourse with them. But his last act is the one deserving unqualified condemnation. To tear a mother from the bedside of her dead child—to incarcerate her in a prison, while the hands of strangers were performing the last sad rites over the dead, is an act that Christianity could never believe, were the evidence not before us, too forcible for denial, too truthful for contradiction. It is an act that calls for withering rebuke, but we dismiss him with the belief that on the coming of that inevitable *Hereafter*, he will receive the punishment he so well merits.

"My remarks are now concluded, and the prisoner is discharged from custody."

There was deep silence for several minutes, during which Harry looked anxiously in the crowd for his friend; but Alfred was nowhere to be seen. Mrs. Wentworth retained her passive look of indifference, and took no further notice of the curious crowd, which gazed upon her with hearts full of pity and commiseration. Once or twice she slowly raised her hand and pressed her forehead with it, as if it ached. But she spoke no word of complaint, nor did she give any other indication of suffering.

Harry was about to remove her from the court, when there was a bustle in the crowd, and the voice of Alfred was heard calling on those around him to give way. He was followed by Awtry, perfectly unconscious of the cause of his companions agitation.

"Make room there, for God's sake," asked Alfred, pressing through the dense mass of men and women. "Follow me," he continued, speaking to Awtry.

The men nearest to him, perceiving his excitement, generally surmised the truth, and a low murmur ran through the room that it was the prisoner's husband, and a passage was quickly made to where Mrs. Wentworth was sitting.

Awtry heard the words, "it is her husband," and turned back with the intention of leaving, but his arm was quickly seized by Alfred, who, still concealing his intention, simply said, "Come on; I will find a passage for us." He hesitated an instant, but, believing his appearance sufficiently disguised to prevent Mrs. Wentworth from recognizing him, he determined to risk proceeding, in the hope of escaping discovery.

At last Alfred was by the side of his wife—the soldier had met her he loved for the first time in nearly two years. Silently and sadly he gazed at her changed appearance, and the briny tears slowly trickled down the soldier's cheeks as he noted her sunken features. At last he spoke.

"Eva!" he said, in a voice that trembled with emotion, "my wife! my darling wife! do you not know me?"

His voice, full of love, sounded in her ear like the sweetest music ever played by the angels of God. At the sound of her name she turned round and looked anxiously in his face—a moment more, and he had scarcely finished speaking, before she had thrown herself in his arms.

"Alfred! my husband!" she murmured, as she pillowed her head in his bosom, "at last—at last!"

"Oh, Heavenly Father!" exclaimed Alfred, raising her head and gazing fondly at the wan and emaciated features of his wife "*is this* all I find?"

His words were those of anguish, wrung out from a tortured heart. It was not so he expected to meet his wife.

"Rise, darling," he continued, "rise, and let us leave this place—let us go where friends are." She rose up, and leaning on his arm, moved off, when he suddenly confronted Awtry, who had stood with anxious and palpitating heart for the closing of the scene. "Stay awhile, dearest," Alfred went on, as soon as he perceived Awtry, "Look at this man—do you know him?"

Mrs. Wentworth looked at him for some time, but failed to recognize Awtry. "I do not know him," she said, shaking her head.

"This is very strange conduct on your part, Mr. Wentworth," said Awtry, believing himself safe.

"Ha!" exclaimed Mrs. Wentworth, "it is his voice. It is Awtry—there he is—I know him now," and she fainted in her husband's arms.

"Seize that man!" thundered Harry, who was standing near Alfred, "he is a spy."

In an instant, Awtry was secured and hurried of to prison. Mrs. Wentworth was conducted by Harry and her husband to Dr. Humphries', where we leave them for awhile.

CHAPTER TWENTY-NINTH.

THE EYE OF GOD—THE MANIAC WIFE.

Pardon us, kind reader, for digressing for awhile from the sad tale it has been our lot to give you, to remark on the strange fancies which govern the minds of a large majority. So inscrutable do the works of the Almighty appear, that we believe all the ills of this world are evoked by Him for some good end. In a measure this is correct. When sinful mortals are burdened with sorrow and affliction, we can recognize in them the chastening hand of God, for under such weight of suffering the soul is apt to pass through purified of the blackness and corruption which darkened and rendered it odious to the good. Here we see the benefits accruing from trouble and distress. We behold the sinner being punished for his transgression, and to the righteous and good, these afflictions are welcomed as the saving of one more soul from the grasp of hell. But how is it when the innocent suffer? It is not the work of the Eternal. High up in the celestial realms, His eyes are turned towards earth to punish the guilty and reward the innocent, and in His works we find no instance where the hands of adversity and suffering have fallen upon those who deserved reward. Where the guiltless are found suffering, He relieves their necessities, and brings them once more that happiness which they deserve on earth.

Why shall it be always said that when a home of happiness is in an instant hurled from the summit of earthly felicity and buried in the dark gulf of adversity, that such is the work of God? If that home is contaminated by grievous sins, there is justice in the claim, but where the transgressions are not heavier than those good men commit, it cannot be, for the God who reigns above seeks to build up, and not to destroy, unless there is no other way of punishing the sinner but by the infliction of the heaviest penalties. We have painted a soldier's wife, if not free from sin, at least innocent of crimes which are calculated to bear upon the conscience and cause remorse or fear; we have pictured her two children, pure and unsinful, for it cannot be said that mortal can sin in infancy. We have shown them plunged in direst misfortunes, and is there not force in the question when we ask if their months of penury and suffering were the works of the God of Mercy and Righteousness?

It cannot be. The innocent do not suffer by the hands of God, while the guilty revel in all the wealth and affluence that this earth bestows. How many men are there who live in ease and comfort, while their souls are burdened with sins? The hypocrite, the liar, the thief, the murderer; all, and by hundreds they can be counted, appear to the world

"A combination and a form, indeed, Where every god did seem to set his seal,"

but in whose souls the fires of hell rage with remorseless fury. But their afflictions are not known to man. The eyes of the world gaze not on them, when the mind is racked by the conflict of sin. We see not their sufferings; we know not the pangs they feel; we only recognize them by the outward appearance. They live, surrounded with all that can make mortal happy, save the happiness of a clear conscience. In this world they prosper, and many gain the applause and commendation of their fellow mortals. What are their sufferings? They are unknown to man, though remembered by God. And if punishment comes at last, it is just and merited, nor do we regret that sin is scourged by the avenging hand of a Savior.

But while we witness the guilty revelling in wealth and affluence, how often are the innocent plunged in want? Aye, myriads of times. We know not of them, but over the land there are hundreds of our fellow mortals whose days are but a repetition of suffering. Famine and sickness have stalked in the midst of hundreds who are innocent of crime, and reduced them to the last brink of despair. Is this the work of God? Forbid it, Heaven! that the charge should be made. There is no ground on which to assert that the Ruler of the Universe—the God of Righteousness—the Lord of Mercy, would thrust the innocent into woe—would blast their earthly prospects—would dash the cup of happiness from their lips, and leave them to perish through Famine and Disease—while men steeped in crime, whose consciences, if read, would show an appalling blackness of guilt—while they, we say, escaped from earthly punishment and enjoyed all the good of this world! On Earth, as in Heaven and Hell, man is divided into two bodies, Angels and Fiends. Both are known to the Almighty, and it is only when His eyes are turned from the good that Fiends triumph. Only then—it is not His work—it cannot and can never be.

And now, kind reader, you may think that the writer is either a lunatic or a madman to advance a doctrine which claims that God—the Infinite—the Everlasting—the Omnipotent—the Inscrutable, would turn awhile from the good and survey them not—allow them to suffer. We are neither the one nor the other. Perchance our doctrine is a mere vagary; still, as we glance over our country and see the scenes daily enacted, we cannot believe they are the work of an Almighty Father. When our maidens are ravished by the hated foe and despoiled of that Virtue held sacred in Heaven, is it the work of God? When the creeping babe is immolated by the savages of the North, is it a dispensation of Providence? When the homesteads of the people are given to the flames and the cursed army of Abolitionists exult at their demolition, does the hand of our Heavenly Father direct the work of destruction? When our temples are profaned by the bacchanalian orgies of the Northern hordes, does the Infinite invite them to desecrate His altars? They are not His works—they never were. These acts which the Christian world shudders at, are the machinations and promptings of Hell, and the Fiends who dwell therein triumph for awhile where the Eye of God is not.

But the Eye of God is not always turned away from His suffering people. The cry of the wretched is borne to His ear by the angels, and Mercy, Charity and Goodness descend to Earth and sweep away the incarnate spirits infesting it. In this we behold the Greatness and Righteousness of God, for though He may see not our hardships for awhile, the cry of the Innocent will ascend to Heaven; their sufferings will be obliterated, and if even on earth they gain not happiness, in those realms where sinless Angels abide, all past woes, all past years of want, all former wretchedness, are removed and forgotten, in an eternity of peace and celestial felicity.

And so it was with the soldier's wife whose sad trials we are narrating to the reader. The spirit of the angel daughter had winged its flight to the Savior, and the little invisible hand pointed to its mother on earth below, and the Son of God supplicated the Father to relieve the miseries of the innocent. We have shown how this was done. The good of earth was the medium of salvation, and her trials are at an end.

Yes, they are at an end! But with them, when she fell fainting in her husband's arms on recognizing Awtry, the light of reason expired, and the soldier's wife was a maniac.

They bore her gently to the residence of Dr. Humphries, and there all that medical science could perform was done, and every attention was lavished upon her. But it was of no avail; madness had seized the mind of Mrs. Wentworth, and the doctor shook his head sadly as he gazed upon her. Days passed on, and still she continued in this state.

"I fear she will only recover her reason to die," observed Dr. Humphries to Harry. "Could her constitution sustain the frenzied excitement she now labors under, I would have some hope, but the months of wretchedness she has passed through, has so weakened her frame that nothing remains but a wreck of what was once a healthy woman."

"This is bad news," remarked Harry, "and I fear it will have a sad effect upon Alfred. I have been overcome with sympathy at observing his silent grief at the bedside of his raving wife, and several times I have heard him mutter, 'never mind, my darling, you will soon recover, and then we will be happy.' Unfortunate man! Could there be the slightest possibility of saving his wife, I am certain you would not despair."

"I do not yet despair," replied the doctor, "although I fear very much her case is hopeless. I have sent for Dr. Mallard and Dr. Purtell; when they have seen Mrs. Wentworth, we will have a consultation, and I trust some good will accrue from it. By the way," he continued, changing the conversation, "have you heard what has become of the supposed spy arrested in the court house?"

"I heard on yesterday that his trunks had been searched, but nothing had been discovered in them, beyond the fact that he was Mr. Awtry, and not an Englishman, as he pretended to be."

"Have they discharged him?" inquired the doctor.

"Oh no;" Harry replied, "the fact of his assuming a false character was deemed sufficient evidence to keep him in prison until further discoveries are made."

"It is very likely, then, that he will eventually pay the penalty of his crimes," observed the doctor.

"Yes; and I trust it will not be long before he suffers death," Harry answered, and then added: "I am not bloodthirsty, nor do I favor the hoisting of the black flag, as so many appear desirous of doing. But for a wretch like Awtry, I have not the slightest pity, and would hear of his execution with pleasure. If even there is no proof discovered of his being a spy, his brutality to Mrs. Wentworth merits punishment, and if only for that, I should desire to see him hung or shot. However, I have no fear but that the fact of his being a spy will be discovered, for several of the most expert detectives in the service are on the search for the necessary evidence to convict him."

"And which evidence I trust they will soon discover," remarked the doctor. "Like you, I am averse to a war of extermination, but when instances like the one before us are brought to our notice, an outraged and indignant people demand satisfaction and should have it accorded to them."

"Ah! my dear sir," replied Harry, "while Awtry's outrage on Mrs. Wentworth deserves condemnation and punishment, he is not solely the guilty cause of her sufferings. From the moment she reached our lines, it was the duty of the people of this city to aid and succor her. Had this been done, her daughter may have been alive this day. Unfortunately the philanthropic and charitable were idle and waited until such cases came to their notice. Had they looked for them, Mrs. Wentworth never would have fallen into the hands of unprincipled speculators and extortioners, and would have been spared the load of affliction which has now periled her life."

"You are right, Harry," said Dr. Humphries. "It is our duty to search for the unfortunate poor, and not to wait until they appeal for assistance. There are many destitute women and children in our midst who have been driven from their once happy and prosperous homes by the hated Yankees. Among them are many high-toned and respectable families, whose pride shrinks from begging for bread, and who now live a life of penury and starvation rather than become the mendicant. And if even they bury delicacy at the mandate of stern Want, they are so apt to be refused assistance by the heartless, that they imagine all of our people alike, and fearing further refusal, shrink with natural horror from a second rejection."

"This can be prevented," observed Harry. "Let the benevolent make it a business to find out the suffering who are worthy of assistance, and let such aid be given, not as charity, but as a duty we owe those who have remained faithful to our cause, and abandoned their homes rather than submit to the enemy. By so doing, we not only alleviate hardships, but we render the soldier happy and contented to serve his country. The knowledge that his family is protected by those at home, and supplied with all that is necessary, will remove from his mind all anxiety for their welfare. It will, besides, grasp them from the clutches of the wretches who are speculating and extorting, and will not only be an act of everlasting honor to those who perform this good work, but will aid our cause as much as if the parties were serving in the field. Many a man who now lies in the deserter's dishonored grave, would have been this day sharing the glory of his country and been looked upon as a patriot, had not his starving wife and children forced him in an evil hour to abandon his post and go to them. It is true, there is no excuse for the deserter, but where the human affections are concerned, it is but natural that the soldier will feel solicitous for the comfort of his wife and children."

"Something of that sort should, indeed, be done," remarked the doctor, "and I believe there are many in our midst who would cheerfully aid in this good work. I cannot believe that the majority of our people are such inhuman characters as Elder and Swartz. It is true that these men have a monopoly in our midst, so far as wealth is concerned, but it would be wrong to blame the majority for the crimes of a few."

"The majority, if even good and charitable, are to blame," replied Harry, firmly, "for if they outnumber the miserable creatures whose sole thought is to amass wealth from the sufferings of our country, it is their duty to thwart such desires by every possible means, and it could be done were the proper steps taken. But they have heretofore displayed an indifference almost criminal, and appear to participate in the unworthy prejudice against refugees. Forgetful that they may to-morrow be similarly situated, they lend a moral, if not an active aid, in the oppression of this unfortunate portion of our people, and are perfectly careless whether want and misery overtake them or not. We must not forget that these refugees are as much entitled to a home in this as in their own State. Their husbands, fathers and brothers are fighting to protect us from subjugation, and if we are unmindful of the comfort of their relatives, it not only entails disgrace upon our name, but renders us deserving of a similar fate, and worse treatment."

"I agree with you," said the doctor, "and so far as I am concerned, everything that can be done for them shall be performed, and—"

Here a knock at the door interrupted the conversation. Harry opened it, and Drs. Mallard and Purtell were announced.

"Good morning to you, gentlemen," said Dr. Humphries, as soon as they entered. "I am very glad you have answered my call so promptly. The case I desire you to see is one of great seriousness, but I withhold any opinion until you have seen the patient and expressed your ideas about it."

"I Suppose it is the lady who was accused of theft," said Dr. Mallard.

"Yes sir," answered Harry, "it is the same person."

"I observed her features very attentively during the trial," remarked Dr. Mallard, "and so convinced was I that she would soon be insane, that I determined, in the event of her being found guilty, to have her released and placed under my care on that plea. Is she raving?" he added inquiringly of Dr. Humphries.

"Yes," replied that gentleman, "but in her ravings she makes no allusion whatever to her wretched life of the past few months. She fancies herself at home in New Orleans again, and as all was then happiness with her, so does everything appear to her mind the reflex of her past days."

"We had better see her now," said Dr. Purtell, "for the sooner something is done towards restoring her reason the better."

"Certainly," answered Dr. Humphries, "walk this way," he continued, leading them toward Mrs. Wentworth's chamber.

At the door he was met by Emma, who had been watching by the bedside of the maniac all the morning.

"Walk easily," she whispered as the three gentlemen appeared at the door. "She is now calmer than ever, but the slightest noise will excite her again."

The medical gentlemen entered the room with noiseless steps, and remained for several minutes watching the sleeping sufferer. Her emaciated features were flushed from excitement and her breathing was hard and difficult. In her sleep, she softly murmured words which told of happy years that were past and vanished forever and could never more return. The broken sentences told of love and happiness, and a deep feeling of sympathy stole into the breasts of her hearers as they listened to her ravings. Alfred was sitting by the bed looking on the wreck of his wife, and when the doctors entered, he arose and briefly saluted them. To their words of condolence he made no reply, for his heart was bitter with grief, and he felt that consolatory language was a mockery, and however well meant and sincere it may have been, it could not relieve the agony he felt at witnessing the destruction of his family's happiness. Oh, let those alone who have felt the burning of the heart when it was wrung with agony, appreciate the misery of men struck down from the pedestal of earthly joy and buried in the gulf of wretchedness. We have known homes where the heart beat high with joy, and life promised to be a future of happiness and peace; where the fairest flowers of affection seemed to bloom for us, and over our pathway floated its perfume, while before our sight, its loveliness remained undiminished until that fatal delusion, Hope, intoxicated the senses and made us oblivions to reality. A brief spell—a charm of short duration, and the hallucination is dispelled, only to leave us seared and blasted, almost hating mankind, and wearing the mask of the hypocrite, leading a double life, to hide the sears left by unsuccessful ambition, or disappointed aspiration. What were death itself compared with the misery of finding, when too late, that the hopes and happiness we deemed reality, were but a shadow, not a substance, which lingered for awhile and Left us to curse our fate.

And yet it is but life—one hour on the pinnacle, the other on the ground. But to our tale.

After remaining by the bedside for several minutes, the doctors were about to leave, when Mrs. Wentworth awoke from her sleep, and gazed with an unmeaning look upon the gentlemen. She recognized no one—not even her husband, who never left her, save when nature imperatively demanded repose.

The doctors requested that Alfred and Emma would retire while they examined the patient. In accordance with their wishes, they did so, and Alfred, entering the balcony, paced up and down, impatient for the result of the consultation. The door of Mrs. Wentworth's chamber remained closed for nearly half an hour, when it opened, and Drs. Humphries, Mallard and Purtell issued from it, looking grave and sad.

The heart of the husband sank as he looked at their features.

"Let me know the worst," he said, huskily, as they approached him.

"We will not deceive you," replied Dr. Mallard, "your wife, we fear, will remain a maniac while her strength lasts, and then—" here he paused.

"And then—" replied Alfred, inquiringly.

"We fear she will only recover her reason to die" continued Dr. Mallard in a tone of sympathy.

"God help, me," uttered the soldier, as he sunk on a chair and buried his face in his hands.

After a few more words full of sympathy and condolence the two doctors left, and shortly after Dr. Humphries dispatched a servant to bring the little boy from the old negro's cabin.

"His presence may rally Mr. Wentworth," the doctor observed to Harry. "Since the consultation he has remained in the same seat, and has never once visited the room of his wife. Something must be done to rouse him from his grief, otherwise it will be fatal to his health."

"The presence of his son may be beneficial," said Harry, "but I do not believe the child can while him away from the sorrow he has met with. It has been a hard—a fatal blow, and has fallen with fearful effect upon my poor friend."

In about an hour the servant returned with the child. He had been neatly dressed in a new suit of clothes and looked the embodiment of childish innocence.

Taking him by the hand Dr. Humphries led him into the balcony where Alfred still sat with his face buried in his hands, deep in thought and racked with grief.

"Here," said the old gentleman, "here is your son. The living and well claim your attention as well as those who are gone and those who suffer."

Alfred raised his head and gazed at the child for a moment.

"My boy," he exclaimed at last, "you are the last link of a once happy chain." As he spoke he pressed the child to his bosom, and the strong-hearted soldier found relief in tears.

CHAPTER THIRTIETH.

DEATH OF THE SOLDIER'S WIFE.

The presence of his child lightened but did not remove the grief of Alfred Wentworth. The love he bore his wife may be likened to the love of the eagle for liberty. Cage it, and the noble bird pines away; no longer allowed to soar on high, but fettered by man, it sickens and dies, nor can it be tamed sufficiently to become satisfied with the wires of a cage. So it was with the soldier. His love for his wife was of so deep and fathomless a nature, that the knowledge of her being a maniac, and only returning to reason to die, changed the current of his nature, and from being a friendly and communicative man, he became a silent and morose being. The world had lost its charms, and the blank left in his heart, the sear upon his mind, the agony at knowing that his wife—his pure and peerless wife, had been compelled from her necessities to take that which was not her own, could never be filled, never be healed and never be eased.

A wife! We know not from experience what it means, but there is a something, an inward voice, which tells, us that a wife is the holiest gift of God to man. A wife! what is it? A woman to cherish and protect, to give the heart's affection to, and to receive all the confiding love with which her bosom is filled. The partner of your happiness—the source of all that makes man good and binds him to earth; the solace of woes, the sharer of joys— the gentle nurse in sickness, and the fond companion in health. Oh! there is a something in the name, which thrills the heart, and makes it beat with emotion at the sound of the word. Amid the cares and pleasures of man, there can be no higher, no worthier desire than to share his triumphs with a wife. When Ambition tempts him to mount yet higher in this earthly life, and take his stand among the exalted men of genius, who so fitting to be the partner of his fame as the gentle woman of this world, and when disappointed in his aspirations, when the cold frowns of a callous world drive him from the haunts of men, who so soothing as a Wife? She will smoothen the wrinkles on his forehead, and by words of loving cheer inspire him with courage and bid him brave the censure and mocking of the world, and strive again to reach the summit of his desires. A Wife! There is no word that appeals with greater force to the heart than this. From the moment the lover becomes the Wife, her life becomes a fountain of happiness to a husband, which gushes out and runs down the path of Time, never to cease, until the power of the Invisible demands and the Angel of Death removes her from his side. Age meets them hand in hand, and still imbued with a reciprocity of affection, her children are taught a lesson from herself which makes the Wife, from generation to generation, the same medium of admiration for the world, the same object of our adoration and homage. We write these lines with homage and respect for the Wife, and with an undefined emotion in our hearts, which tells us they are correct, and that the value of a Wife is all the imagination can depict and the pen indite.

And to lose one! Oh! what sorrow it must awaken—how the fountains of grief must fill to overflowing, when the companion of your life is torn from you by the hand of Death! No wonder, then, that the heart of Alfred Wentworth bled with woe, and he became a changed man. What cared he longer for this world? Almost nothing! But one thing urged him to rally his energies and meet the blow with fortitude whenever it should come. It was the knowledge that his little boy would need a father's care. This made him not quite oblivious to this world, for though his life would be in the front, so soon as he returned to the battle-field, there were chances for his escaping death, and his desire was to live, so that the child might grow up and remind him of his wife. No, not remind! As fresh as the hour when love first entered his heart for her—as plain as the day he led her to the altar and registered his vows to Heaven—and as pure as herself, would his memory ever be for her. Time can soothe woes, obliterate the scars left by grief, but the memory of a dead wife can never be extinguished in the mind of a husband, even though her place in his heart may be filled by another. She must ever be recollected by him, and each hour he thinks of her, so will her virtues shine brighter and more transparent, and her faults, if any, become forgotten, as they were forgiven. But we weary the reader with these digressions, and will proceed to close our narrative.

Three additional weeks passed, and still Mrs. Wentworth remained insane, but her insanity being of a gentle character, Dr. Humphries would not permit her to be sent to the lunatic asylum, as her husband advised. It is true, he desired it more for the purpose of avoiding being the recipient of any further favors, than because he thought it necessary. This morbid sensitiveness shrank from being obligated to a comparative stranger like the doctor, and it was not until the old gentleman absolutely refused to permit Mrs. Wentworth to leave the house, that he yielded his assent to her remaining.

"As you insist upon it," he remarked, "I make no further opposition to her remaining, but I think it an imposition on your benevolence that your home shall be made gloomy by my wife being in it."

"Not in the least gloomy, sir," replied the doctor, "nor do I think it the slightest imposition upon my benevolence. Were it only to repay the debt Harry owes you for the preservation of his life, I should insist upon her not being removed. But I deem it a duty we owe to our suffering fellow mortals, and as long as she remains in her present state, so long will she be an inmate of my house, and everything that can lighten and ameliorate her unhappy condition shall be deemed a pleasant business to perform."

"I do not doubt it, sir," said Alfred, grasping the doctor's hand and shaking it heartily, "believe me, the attention of your daughter, Harry and yourself, has been the oasis in my present desert of life, and though in a few short weeks I expect all will be over, and she will no longer need your care, the memory of your kindness in these gloomy times of sorrow, shall ever remain unfading in memory, and shall always be spoken of and thought of with the greatest gratitude."

"No gratitude is necessary," answered the doctor as he returned the pressure of Alfred Wentworth's hand, "I consider myself performing a sacred duty, both to God and to humanity, and no gratitude is needed for the faithful performance of the same."

"No, no sir," interrupted Alfred, hastily, "it is no duty, and cannot be looked upon as such—at least by me."

"Well, well," remarked the doctor, "we will not argue about that. I only wish it were in my power to do more by giving you assurance that your wife will recover, but I fear very much she never can."

"How long do you suppose she will linger?" asked Alfred sadly.

"I cannot tell," replied the doctor, "Her strength has been failing very rapidly for the past week, and I do not think she can last much longer."

"Could nothing be done to keep her alive, if even it were as a maniac?" he inquired, and then added, and as he spoke, repressing the emotion he felt, "Could she but live, it would be some solace to me, for then I should have her with me, and by procuring a position in some of the departments, be enabled to remain with her; but the idea of her dying—it is that which saddens me and almost makes me curse the hour I left her. My poor, darling wife!"

The last words were uttered as if he were speaking to himself, and the tone of sorrow in which he spoke touched Dr. Humphries deeply.

"Bear with fortitude the dispensations of a Divine Providence," said the old gentleman. "If He has willed that your wife shall die, you must bow humbly to the decree. Time will assuage your grief and remove from your mind, this sad—too sad fate that has befallen her."

"If you think that time can assuage my grief," replied Alfred, "you greatly underrate the strength of my affection. When a mere stripling, I first met my wife, and from that hour all the affection I possessed was hers. Each day it grew stronger, and at the time I left New Orleans with my regiment, the love I bore my wife, and for her, my children, could not have been bartered for the wealth of California. She was to me a dearer object than all else on earth, and more—"

He could speak no longer, so overcome was he with emotion. Once more wringing the doctor's hand, he left the room and entered the chamber of his wife.

"Unhappy man," exclaimed the doctor, when he was alone, "his is, indeed, a bitter grief, and one not easily obliterated."

With these words the kind-hearted old gentleman retired to his study, greatly moved at the misfortunes of the family he had been brought in contact with.

The furloughs granted to Alfred and Harry had been renewed on the expiration of the time they had been granted for, but on the representation of Dr. Humphries, had been renewed. At the time the above conversation took place, they were again nearly expired and Harry determined to appeal to the government once more for a second renewal. Accordingly he took the cars for Richmond and obtaining an interview with the Secretary of War, he represented the condition of Mrs. Wentworth, and exhibited the certificates of several doctors that she could not survive two months longer. For himself, he requested a further renewal of his furlough on the ground of his approaching marriage. With that kindness and consideration which distinguished Gen. Randolph, his applications were granted, and leaves of absence for Alfred and himself for sixty days longer were cordially granted.

With the furloughs, he arrived from Richmond the same evening that the conversation related above took place between the doctor and Alfred, and on the return of his friend from his wife's chamber, he presented him with his leave.

"You are indeed a friend," remarked Alfred, "and I can never sufficiently repay the kindness you have shown me. But before this furlough expires I do not suppose I shall have any wife to be with."

"Why do you speak so?" inquired Harry.

"She cannot last much longer," he replied. "Although unwillingly and with sorrow I am compelled to acknowledge that every day she sinks lower, and to-day her appearance denotes approaching dissolution too plain, even for me to persuade myself that such is not the case."

"I cannot tell you I hope you are mistaken," observed his friend, "for I feel that such language can never lighten nor remove your sorrow. But be assured that I deeply sympathize with you in your affliction."

"I know it," he answered. "Would to heaven all in the South were like you. It might have been different with my poor wife, and my angel girl might have been alive this day. However, it was not their duty to succor and protect my family, and I have no right to complain because they lent her no helping hand. I alone must bear the weight of my affliction, and from the misery it causes me, I devoutly trust none of my comrades may ever know it. Here your betrothed comes," he continued, observing Emma at the door. "I will leave you for the present, as I suppose you wish to speak with her and I desire to be alone for awhile."

"Do not let her presence hasten your departure," said Harry. "She will be as happy in my company while you are here, as if no third person was present."

Alfred smiled faintly as he replied: "Her presence alone does not impel me to leave, but I desire to be alone for a time. My mind is very much unsettled, and a few moments of solitary thought will restore it to its wonted quietue."

Rising from his seat, he bade Harry adieu, and bowing to Emma, who entered at the moment, left the house and bent his steps toward his lodgings. Dr. Humphries had invited him to be a guest at his house, but he politely but firmly declined the invitation, at the same time his days were spent there with his wife, and it was only in the evening he left, to take a few moments of rest. From the time he discovered his wife, and she was carried to Dr. Humphries' residence, he had never been to any other place than the doctor's or his lodgings.

Four days after Harry's return, he was seated with Emma in the parlor conversing on the subject of his marriage, which the fair girl desired put off until after Mrs. Wentworth's death, which her father told her could not be postponed many weeks. Her lover endeavored to combat her resolution, by declaring that while Alfred would always get a furlough if his wife was still alive at the expiration of its time, he could neither ask nor expect to obtain any further extension. They were in the midst of a warm discussion, when Dr. Humphries entered. He had just come from Mrs. Wentworth's room, and appeared exceedingly sad.

"How is Mrs. Wentworth this morning, father?" inquired Emma, as the doctor entered, and observing his mournful expression, she added, "What is the matter."

"Mrs. Wentworth has recovered her reason, and is dying," he replied.

"Poor Alfred," observed Harry, "this hour will not take him by surprise, but it cannot fail to add to his grief."

"Has he been here this morning," asked the doctor.

"Not yet," answered Harry, "but," he continued, looking at his watch, "he will soon be here, for it is now his usual hour of coming."

"I trust he will not delay," said Dr. Humphries "for his wife cannot last three hours longer."

"In that event, I had better go and look for him," Harry observed "he never leaves his lodgings except to come here, and there will be no difficulty in finding him."

Rising from his seat, he took up his hat and departed for his friend. Before he had gone two squares he met Alfred, and without saying anything to him, retraced his steps to the doctor's window.

"My friend" said Doctor Humphries as Alfred entered, "the hour has come, when you must summon all your fortitude and hear with resignation the stern decree of the Almighty. Your wife is perfectly sane this morning but she is dying. On entering her chamber a while ago, I found her quite composed and perfectly sensible of the life she had passed through. Though she did not recognize me, an intuitive knowledge of who I was, possessed her, and her first request was that you should be sent to her. Your little boy is now with her and she awaits your arrival."

Taking Alfred by the hand and followed by Harry, the doctor led the way to the chamber of the dying wife. The child was sitting on the bed with his mothers arms around his neck. Emma, Elsie, and the old negro were standing at the bedside looking sorrowfully at Mrs. Wentworth. As soon as her husband entered, they made way for him to approach.

"Alfred, my husband" exclaimed Mrs. Wentworth, extending her arms, "I am so glad you have come that I can see you once more before I die."

"Eva, my heart strings are torn with agony to see you thus" he replied raising her gently and pillowing his head on her bosom, "Oh! my wife, that this should be the end of all my hopes. What consolation is there left to me on earth when you are gone."

"Speak not so despairingly" she answered, "It were better that I should die than live with a burning conscience. My husband, the act for which I have been tried, still haunts me, for here on earth it will ever be a reproach, while in Heaven, the sin I committed will be forgiven through the intercession of a divine Savior."

"Perish the remembrance of that act!" answered her husband. "To me my darling wife it can make no difference, for I regret only the necessity which impelled you to do it, and not the act. Live, oh my wife, live and your fair fame shall never suffer, while your husband is able to shield you from the reproaches of the world. Though the proud may affect to scorn you, those in whose hearts beats a single touch of generosity will forgive and forget it, and if even they do not, in the happiness of my unfaltering affections, the opinions of the world, can be easily disregarded."

"It cannot be" she answered, "I am dying Alfred, and before many hours, the spirit will be resting in heaven. To have you by my side ere my breath leaves my body, to grasp your hand, and gaze on your loved features ere I die, removes all my unhappiness of the weary months now past, and I leave this world content."

"Oh my wife" said Alfred, "Is this the end of our married life? Is this the reward I reap for serving my country! Oh, had I remained in New Orleans, the eye of the libertine would never have been cast upon you, and you would have been saved from the grasp of the heartless speculator and extortioner.—What is independence compared with you my wife? What have I gained by severing the ties of love and leaving a happy home, to struggle for the liberty of my country? A dead child—a dying wife—a child who will now be motherless; while I will be a wretched heart-broken man. Better, far better, had I resisted the calls of my country, and remained with you, than to return and find my happiness gone, and my family beggared, and tossing on the rough billows of adversity, unheeded by the wealthy, and unfriended by all."

"Speak not so, my husband," she answered, "my sufferings may be the price of independence, and I meet them cheerfully. Though in my hours of destitution, despair may have caused me to utter words of anguish, never, for a moment, have I regretted that you left me, to struggle for your country. If in my sufferings; if in the death of my child; if in my death; and if in the destroying of our once happy family circle, the cause for which you are a soldier is advanced, welcome them. Woman can only show her devotion by suffering, and though I cannot struggle with you on the battle-field, in suffering as I have done, I feel it has been for our holy cause."

"Eva, Eva," he exclaimed, "do all these give you back to me? Do they restore my angel daughter? Do they bring me happiness? Oh, my wife, I had hoped that old age would meet us calmly floating down the stream of Time, surrounded by a happy family, and thanking God for the blessings he had bestowed upon me. When I first led you to the altar, I dreamed that our lives would be blended together for many, many years, and though I knew that the 'Lord giveth and the Lord taketh away,' and that at any time we may die, I never thought that the end of our happiness would be brought about in such a way as this. You tell me it is the price of Independence. Aye, and it is a fearful price. When you are laid in the cold grave aside of Ella, and I am struggling in the battle-field, what is there to inspire me with courage, and bid me fight on until liberty is won? And when it is at last achieved, I cannot share the joy of my comrades. I have no home to go to, and if even I have, it is desolate. No wife is there to welcome me, no daughter to thank me, but I must take my orphan boy by the hand, and leading him to your grave, kneel by its side and weep together on the sod that covers your remains."

There was not a dry eye in the room. All wept with the husband, and even the dying woman could not restrain the tears.

"Alfred," she said, "do not weep. My husband, up there, in Heaven, we will meet again, and then the desolation on earth will be more than repaid by the pleasure of eternal joy. Let not my death cause you to falter in your duty to the South. Promise me, my husband, that through all changes you will ever remain steadfast and loyal to her sacred cause. Look not on the cruelty of a few men as the work of the whole, and remember that if even you are not made happier by the achievement of independence, there are others you assist in making so, and other homes which would have been as desolate as yours, but for you and your comrades' defense. Promise me, Alfred, that so long as the war lasts, you will never desert the South."

"I promise," he replied.

"There is now but one thing that gives me thought," she continued, her voice growing weaker each moment, "our little boy—"

"Shall have a home so long as I live and his father is serving his country," interrupted Dr. Humphries. "Rest easy on that subject, madam," he continued, "it will be a pleasure for me to take care of the boy."

"Then I die happy," said Mrs. Wentworth, and turning to her husband she said with difficulty, "Farewell, my husband. Amid all my trials and sufferings my love for you has ever been as true and pure as the hour we married. To die in your arms, with my head on your bosom was all I wished, and my desire is gratified. Farewell."

Before her husband could reply her reason had vanished, and she remained oblivious to all around her. Her eyes were closed, and the moving of her lips alone told that she yet lived.

"Eva! darling! Wife!" exclaimed Alfred passionately "Speak to me! oh my angel wife, speak one word to me ere you die. Look at me! say that you recognize me. Awake to consciousness, and let me hear the sound of your voice once more. Wake up my wife" he continued wildly, "Oh for another word—one look before you are no more."

His wild and passionate words reached the ear of the dying woman, and her voice came again, but it was the dying flicker of the expiring lamp. She slowly opened her eyes and looked up in the face of her husband.

"Alfred—husband, happiness" she murmured softly, then gently drawing down his head, her lips touched his for an instant, and the soldier's wife embraced her husband for the last time on earth.

Releasing his head Mrs. Wentworth kept her eyes fixed upon those of her husband. Their glances met and told their tale of deep and unutterable affection. The look they gave each other pierced their souls, and lit up each heart with the fires of love. Thus they continued for several minutes, when Mrs. Wentworth, rising on her elbow, looked for a moment on the grief struck group around her bed.

"Farewell," she murmured, and then gazing at her husband, her lips moved, but her words could not be heard.

Stooping his ear to her lips, Alfred caught their import, and the tears coursed down his cheek.

The words were, "My husband I die happy in your arms."

As if an Almighty power had occasioned the metamorphosis, the countenance of the dying woman rapidly changed, and her features bore the same appearance they had in years gone by. A smile lingered round her lips, and over her face was a beautiful and saint-like expression. The husband gazed upon it, and her resemblance to what she was in days of yore, flashed across his mind with the rapidity of lightning. But the change did not last long, for soon she closed her eyes and loosened her grasp on her husband's neck, while her features resumed their wan and cheerless expression. Nothing but the smile remained, and that looked heavenly. Alfred still supported her; he thought she was asleep.

"She is now in heaven," said Doctor Humphries solemnly.

Yes, she was dead! No more could the libertine prosecute her with his hellish passions; no more could his vile and lustful desires wreak their vengeance on her, because of disappointment. No more could the heartless extortioner turn her from a shelter to perish in the streets. No more could the gardened and uncharitable speculator wring from her the last farthing, nor could suffering and starvation tempt her any more to commit wrong. No—she is in heaven. *There* the libertine is not and can never be. *There* she will ever find a shelter, for *there* the extortioner rules not. There the speculator can never dwell, and in that holy abode suffering and starvation can never be known. An eternity of happiness was now hers. To the home of the Father and to the dwelling of the Son, her spirit had winged its flight, and henceforth, instead of tears, and lamentations the voice of another angel would be heard in Paradise chanting the praises of Jehovah.

Yes, the eye of God was turned upon the soldiers wife, and she was made happy. Her months of grief and misery were obliterated, and the Almighty in his infinite goodness, had taken her to himself—had taken her to Heaven. The spirit of the mother is with the child, and both are now in that home, where we all hope to go. In the ear of the soldier, two angels are whispering words of divine comfort and peace, and as their gentle voice enter his heart, a feeling of resignation steals over this mind, and kneeling over the dead body of his wife he gently murmurs,

"Thy will be done oh God!"

Every voice is hushed, every tear is dried, and the prayer of the soldier ascends to Heaven for strength to hear his affliction. The eye of God is now upon him, and He can minister to the supplicant.

CHAPTER THIRTY-FIRST.

CONCLUSION.

The dead was buried. The hearse was followed by a large concourse of Dr. Humphries' friends, who were brought there by the sad tale of the trials of the Soldier's Wife. The funeral service was read, and after the grave was closed many grouped around Alfred and offered their condolence. He only bowed but made no reply. The body of Ella had been previously disinterred and placed in the same grave which afterward contained her mother, and on the coffins of his wife and child Alfred Wentworth took a last look. When the service was over he turned away, and accompanied by Harry returned to the dwelling of the doctor, where, with his boy on his knees, he conversed.

"My furlough does not expire for forty days," he observed, "but I shall rejoin my regiment in a week from this time. The object for which it was obtained being no longer there, it is only just that I shall report for duty."

"You must do no such thing," answered Harry, "I wish you to remain until your leave expires."

"Why?" asked Alfred, in a tone of surprise.

"Well, the fact is," said Harry, "I will be married in thirty days, and it is my urgent desire that you shall be with me on my marriage day, as a guest, if not as a friend."

"I can make but a poor guest," he replied. "My heart is too full of grief to willingly join in the mirth and happiness such festivities bring with them. You must therefore excuse me. I should indeed start at once did I not desire to find a place to leave this child."

"You need not trouble yourself about him," remarked Harry, "the doctor assured your wife that he should take care of the boy, and I feel certain he will be a father to him during your absence. Nor will I excuse your absence at my wedding, for I do not see why you should object if I desire it, and Emma, I know, will be very much pleased at your presence. So offer no excuses, but prepare yourself to remain."

"As you appear so much to desire it," he answered. "I will remain, but I assure you I feel but little inclined for such pleasure at the present time, particularly a wedding, which cannot fail to bring up reminiscences of a happy day, not so long gone but that it still remains in my memory, as fresh and vivid as when I was an actor in a similar occasion."

"Let not such thoughts disturb you," said Harry, "let the Past bury the Past. Look forward only to the Future, and there you will find objects worthy of your ambition, and if you will pursue them, they will serve to eradicate from your mind the harrowing scene you have just passed through. Believe me, Alfred," he continued, "it will never do to pass your days in vain regrets at what is passed and vanished. It serves to irritate and keep open the wounds in our lives, while it never soothes the afflicted, nor gives us a moment of peace. Let the present and future alone occupy your thoughts. They will give you food for reflection, sufficient to bury all former unhappiness, and to entail upon you a return of that earthly joy you once possessed."

"Your remarks are correct in theory, my friend," replied Alfred, "but they cannot be put into practice. Sooner can the Mississippi river be drained of its waters than the inexorable Past be obliterated from the mind of man. It must ever remain in his memory, and though at times it may lie dormant, the slightest event will be all that is necessary to awake it into life. The cares of the present may deprive it of active participation in the mind; anxiety for the future may prevent the mind of man from actively recurring to it, but it still remains indelibly imprinted on the memory, and though a century of years should pass, and the changes of Time render the Present opposite to the Past, the latter can never be forgotten. Think not that coming years can render me oblivious to my present affliction. They may make dull the agony I now feel, and perchance I will then wear as bright a smile as I did in years ago, but the remembrance of my wife and child will never be blunted; no, nor shall a shade cross over my heart, and dim the affection I had for them, while living, and for their memory now that they are in the grave."

Alfred was right. The words of Harry were a theory which sounds well enough for advice, but which can never be placed into practice. The Past! who can forget it? The Present, with its load of cares; with its hours of happiness and prosperity; with its doubts and anxieties, is not sufficiently powerful to extinguish remembrance of the Past. The Future, to which we all look for the accomplishment of our designs—the achievement of our ambitious purposes—cannot remove the Past. Both combined are unequal to the task, and the daily life of man proves it so.

The Past! what a train of thought does it suggest! Aye, the Past, with its pleasures and misfortunes. It haunts our consciences, and is ever before our eyes. The murderer, though safely concealed from the world, and who may have escaped punishment by man for years, still has the Past to confront and harass his mind. Penitence and prayer may lighten, but can never remove it. Surrounded though he be with health and happiness, the demon of the Past will confront him ever, and make his life wretched. Oh, what a fearful thing is that same Past, we hear spoken of lightly by those whose lives have been along a smooth and flowery track over the same, and unmarked by a single adversity or crime. A single deviation from the path of honor, integrity and virtue, and as years roll on the memory of those past hours will cause bitter self-reproach, for it will be irremovable. So with past happiness as it is with misery and crime. The beggar can never forget his past joys in contemplating the present or hoping for the future, but it must ever remain a source of never-failing regret and the fountain of unhealable wounds.

The Past!—but no more of it, as we write the recollection of past happiness and prosperity, of past follies and errors rise up with vividness, and though it is never forgotten, burns with a brighter light than before.

Several days after his conversation with Harry, Alfred received a message from Dr. Humphries requesting him to meet that gentleman at ten o'clock the same morning at his residence. Accordingly, at the appointed hour, he presented himself to the Doctor, by whom he was received with great cordiality and kindness.

"I have sent for you, Mr. Wentworth," began the doctor, as soon as Alfred was seated, "to speak with you on a subject which interests you as well as myself. As you are aware, I promised your wife when she was dying that your remaining child should never want a home while I lived. This promise I now desire you to ratify by gaining your consent to his remaining with me, at least until he is old enough not to need the care of a lady."

"You have placed me under many obligations already, Dr. Humphries," replied Alfred, "and you will pardon me if I feel loath to add another to the already long list. I have already formed a plan to place my child in the hands of the Sisters of Charity at Charleston, by whom he will be treated with the greatest kindness, and with but small expense to myself. You must be aware that as a soldier my pay is very small, while I have no opportunity of increasing my salary by engaging in any mercantile pursuit. Such being the case, and as I could not consent to your defraying the expenses of the child, I think it better for him to be where I shall need only a small sum of money to pay all needed charges. At the same time let me assure you of my sincere gratitude for your generous offer."

"I will not hear of your objections, my good friend," said the doctor; "it is my desire that you allow me to adopt the boy, if only in part. My daughter will shortly be married, as you are aware, and then I shall be left alone. I possess ample means, and would not accept a dollar in return for the expenses incurred for the child, while his presence will be a source of happiness to me. Already I have formed an attachment for him, and it will only be gratifying my sincere wish if you will give your consent. Believe me, I do not ask it for the purpose of laying you under any obligations, or from any charitable motive, but from an earnest desire for him to remain with me. Let me hope that you will give your consent."

"I scarcely know what to say," answered Alfred, "for while I feel a natural delicacy in giving my consent, my heart tells me that the child will be far more comfortable than if he were at the convent."

"Why then do you not give your consent in the same spirit the offer is made," observed the doctor. "My dear sir," he continued, "let no false idea of delicacy prevent you from giving your consent to that, which cannot fail to render your child happy and comfortable."

"I cannot give a decided answer to-day" said Alfred. "You will give me time to consider your offer—say a week. In the meantime I have no objection to my child remaining with you until my mind is decided upon what course I shall pursue."

"I suppose I must be satisfied to wait" answered doctor Humphries, "but let me trust your decision will be a favorable one." As I remarked before, I desire you consent, from none but the purest motives, and I hope you will grant it.

The sad tale with which we have endeavored to entertain the reader is over. To the writer it has been no pleasant task, but the hope that it may prove of some service, and of some interest to the public has cheered us in our work, and disposed us to endure its unpleasantness. Apart from the dearth of literary productions in the South, we have believed that a necessity existed for a work of this nature, and with such belief we have given the foregoing pages to the people, in the hope that it may prove, not merely a novel to be read, criticised and laid aside, but to be thought over, and its truth examined, in the daily lives of hundreds in our midst. It is true, that with the license of all writers we may have embellished misery *as a whole* to a greater extent than reality, but if it is taken to pieces no exaggeration will be discovered, and each picture drawn herein will be found as truthful as our pen has depicted.

As the reader may desire to know what become of the principal characters remaining, we anticipated their desire, by making enquiry, and learned the following facts, which we give to make this work as complete as possible.

Thirty days after the burial of Mrs. Wentworth, a large assemblage of gaily dressed ladies and gentlemen assembled at the residence of doctor Humphries to witness the marriage of Emma. The party was a brilliant one; the impressive ceremony of the Episcopal church was read, and Harry Shackleford was the husband of Emma Humphries. The usual amount of embracing and congratulation occurred on the occasion, after which the party adjourned to the dining room, where a sumptuous supper had been prepared, and which was partaken of by the guests with many compliments to the fair bride and bridegroom, while many toasts were offered and drank, wishing long life, health and prosperity to the young couple. The party lasted to a late hour in the night, when the guests dispersed, all present having spent their hours in gaiety and happiness.

No, not all, for apart from the throng, while the marriage ceremony was being read, was one who looked on the scene with a sad heart. Clad in deep mourning, and holding his child, by the hand, Alfred Wentworth standing aloof from the crowd saw Emma and his friend united as man and wife with deep emotion. It had been only a few years before, that he led his wife to the altar and the reminiscences of the present awoke, and stirred his grief, and brought back upon him, with the greatest force, his sad bereavement. A tear started to his eyes, as he thought of his present unhappiness, and he turned aside, to hide his emotion from the crowd. Dashing the tear away, he offered his congratulation and good wishes to the newly married couple, as he thought, with calmness, but the quiver of his lips as he spoke, did not pass unperceived by Harry, and as he clasped the extended hand of his friend, a feeling of sympathy, which he could afford even in his happiness, crept over him.

Shortly after his marriage, Harry returned to his command, and is now the Lieutenant Colonel of his regiment, having been promoted to that honorable position for gallantry exhibited on many battle fields. When last we heard of him he was on furlough, and with his wife in Alabama, where they now reside, he having removed to that State a short time previous to the fall of Vicksburg. So far, his wedded life has been one of unalloyed happiness, and we can only wish that it may continue so, through many long years. To his wife, though she has not been a very prominent character in this book, we tender our best wishes for the continuance of that happiness she now enjoys, and trust the day will soon arrive when her husband will have no farther need to peril his life in defence of his country, but turning his sword into a plough, be enabled to live always with her, and to require no more "furloughs."

Shortly after his daughter's marriage and removal to Alabama, Doctor Humphries found Jackson too lonely for him to reside at. He therefore, removed into the same State, where he possessed a plantation, and is now residing there, beloved and respected by all who know him. The unfortunate life of Mrs. Wentworth, and the sad fate of herself and the little Ella, did not fail to make him actively alive to the duties of the wealthy towards those who were driven from their homes by the enemy, and compelled to seek refuge in the States held by the Confederate government. Every time a refugee arrived at his locality he visits the unfortunate family with a view to finding out the state of their circumstances. If he discovers they are in need, relief is immediately granted, and the parties placed above want. By his energy and perseverance he has succeeded in forming a society for the relief of all refugees coming into the country, and as President of the same, has infused a spirit of benevolence in the members, which promises to become a blessing to themselves as well as to the wretched exiles who are in their midst.

The little Alfred is still with the Doctor, and is a source of much pleasure to the old gentleman. It was only after the greatest persuasions possible that his father consented to his remaining, but being overcome by the argument of the Doctor and Harry as well as the solicitations of Emma, he at last gave his consent, feeling at the same time that his boy would be happier and fare more comfortable than with the Sisters of Mercy, who, from their austere and religious life, are ill suited to rear an infant of such tender years. The boy is happy and can every evening be seen setting on the knees of Doctor Humphries, who he calls "grandfather" and indulging in innocent prattle. He has not yet forgotten his mother and sister, and very often he enquires of the Doctor if they will not come back to him at some future time. On these occasions the old gentleman shakes his head, and tells him that they are gone to heaven where he will meet them at some future time, if he behaves like a good boy. Enjoying good health and perfectly happy, although anxious for the termination of the war, and the achievement of our independence, we leave this worthy gentleman, with the hope that he may long live to receive the blessings and thanks of those who are daily benefited by his philanthropic benevolence.

The good old negro and Elsie accompanied the Doctor to Alabama, and are now residing on the Doctor's plantation. The old woman still resides in a cabin by herself, for no amount of persuasion could induce her to stay at the residence, but every day she may be seen hobbling to the house with some present for the little Alfred. The clothes which little Ella died in, and the remainder of the wedding gown, are kept sacredly by her, and often she narrates, to a group of open-mouthed negro children, the sad tale of the soldier's wife, embellishing, as a matter of course, the part she had in the eventful drama. Her kindness to Mrs. Wentworth and Ella, was not forgotten by the soldier, and before he left for the army, she received a substantial reward as a token of his gratitude. She often speaks of Ella as the little angel who "was not feared to die, case she was a angel on earf."

Notwithstanding he had yielded to so many offers of the Doctor, Alfred would not consent to receive Elsa from him, unless he paid back the sum of money given for the girl. This he could not do at the time, and it was decided that she should remain as the slave of Doctor Humphries, until he could refund the amount. She is now serving exclusively as the nurse of the little boy, and is as happy and contented as any slave in the South. Her attachment to the child increases daily, and nothing in the world could induce her to forego the pleasure of attending to her wants. The old negro and herself are often together, conversing of the unfortunate family of her former master, and their remarks teem with sympathy and abound with the affection felt by every slave for a kind and indulgent owner. Although of a servile race, we leave these negroes, regretting that in the hearts of many of our white people the same generous feelings do not exist. It is sad to think that, with all the advantages of birth, education, and position, there should be found men of Caucasian origin, who are below the negro in all the noble attributes of mankind. But there are many such, and while they do not elevate the servile race, they lower, to a considerable degree, the free born and educated.

Vicksburg fell on the fourth day of July, 1863, and the anniversary of American independence was celebrated by the Yankees in a Southern city which had cost them thousands of lives to capture. A few days after the surrender, the enemy advanced on Jackson, and compelled General Johnston to evacuate that city, to save his army. These are matters of history, and are doubtless well known to the reader. After retaining possession a short time, the Yankees retreated from the place, but not before they had given another proof of the vandalism for which they have been rendered infamous throughout the civilized world, by setting the city on fire. Luckily only a portion of the town was destroyed, and we could almost rejoice at being able to write that among the many buildings burnt were those belonging to Mr. Elder. Did not the homes of many good and worthy men share the same fate, we would almost attribute the destruction of his property to the righteous indignation of God. He lost every residence he possessed, and as the insurance companies refused to renew, from the aspect of affairs, on the expiration of his policies, the loss was a total one, and reduced him to almost beggary. With a few negroes he reached Mobile and is now living on the income their labor yields. His brutal conduct had reached the Bay city, before the fall of Jackson, and on his arrival there, instead of receiving the sympathy and aid of the generous hearted people, he was coldly met and all rejoiced at his downfall. Those, in that city, who in heart were like him, might have offered assistance, did they not fear that such conduct would lead to suspicion and eventuate the exposition of their enormities. His punishment is the just reward for his iniquities, and we record almost with regret that he is not reduced to abject beggary. Though we are told to "return good for evil" and to "forgive our enemies," we cannot in the case of Mr. Elder do either, but would like very much to see the Mosaic law of "an eye for an eye and a tooth for a tooth" put in force, and in this wish those who are even more charitable than ourselves will coincide.

Swartz is now in Augusta, Georgia, living in ease and affluence, like the majority of Southern speculators. The lesson he received from his uncharitableness, has not benefited him in the slightest degree. He still speculates on the wants of the poor, and is as niggardly to the needy. Though loyal to the Confederacy, we believe his loyalty only caused from his being the possessor of a large amount of Confederate funds, but perhaps we judge him wrongfully. At any rate, he has never done any act, either for the government or for individuals to merit praise or approbation. In justice to the Germans of the South, we would state that when his conduct towards Mrs. Wentworth became known, they generally condemned him.—As we observed in a former chapter, kindness and benevolence is the general trait of the Germans, and we would not have it supposed that Swartz is a representative of that people. The loss sustained by Mr. Swartz, by the fall of Jackson, was comparatively insignificant, and therefore he has felt no change of fortune. The punishment that he merits, is not yet meted to him, but we feel certain that it will be dealt to him at the proper time.

Further investigation and search resulted in the discovery of sufficient evidence to convict Awtry of being a spy. When brought before the court martial convened to try him, he displayed considerable arrogance, and obstinately persisted in declaring himself a British subject. With such plausibility did he defend himself, that the court was at first very much puzzled to decide whether or not he was a spy, for every evidence brought against the prisoner was explained and made insignificant by his consummate skill in argument, and it was only by the opportune arrival of a detective with the most decided proof of his guilt, that he was condemned to death. Awtry received the sentence of the court with haughty indifference, and was led back to prison, to await death by hanging. On the morning of his execution, the courage and obstinacy which had sustained him from the day of his arrest, gave way, and to the minister who edited upon him, he made a full confession of his having been sent to Mississippi as a spy for Sherman, and that he had already supplied that yankee General with valuable information of the strength and capacity of Vicksburg for resistance. He was very much humiliated at being condemned to death by hanging and made application for the sentence to be changed to shooting, but the military authorities declined acceding to his demand, and he was accordingly hanged on the branches of a tree near Jackson. A small mound of earth in an obscure portion of the Confederacy is all that is left to mark the remains of Horace Awtry. The libertine and prosecutor of Mrs. Wentworth is no more, and to God we leave him. In His hands the soul of the dead will be treated as it deserves, and the many sins which stain and blacken it will be punished by the Almighty as they deserve. Black as was his guilt, we have no word of reproach for the dead. Our maledictions are for the living alone, and then we give them only when stern necessity demands it, and when we do, our work of duty is blended with regret, and would be recalled were it possible, and did not the outraged imperatively demand it. To our Savior, we leave Awtry Before the Judge of mankind he will be arraigned for his guilty acts on earth, and the just voice of the Father, will pronounce on him the punishment he merits.

But one more character remains for us to notice. Three or four times in the last twelve months a man dressed in the uniform of a Lieutenant of the Staff, and wearing a black crape around his arm, may have been seen with a little boy kneeling by the side of a grave in the cemetery of Jackson, Mississippi. The grave contains two remains, but is covered over with one large brick foundation from which ascends a pure and stainless shaft of marble, with the following inscription on its snowy front:

SACRED TO THE MEMORY OF

MY WIFE AND CHILD,

EVA AND ELLA WENTWORTH.
"Their troubles o'er, they rest in peace."
1863.

A.W.

As our readers must perceive, the stranger and child, are Alfred Wentworth and his little boy. About four months after the death of his wife, he was appointed Inspector General of a Louisiana brigade with the rank of first Lieutenant, and being stationed for awhile near Jackson, paid frequent visits to the city, and never failed on such occasions to take his son to the grave of his wife and child. There, kneeling before the grave, the broken hearted soldier would offer up a prayer to God for the repose of the souls of those beneath the sod. The tears which fell on the grave on such visits, and watered the last resting place of the loved ones were the holiest that ever flowed from the eyes of man—they were the homage of a bereaved husband to the memory of a pure and spotless wife, and an angel daughter. Alfred is still alive, and has passed unharmed through many a hard fought battle. Those who know not the tale of his family's sufferings and unhappy fate, think him moody and unfriendly, but those who are acquainted with the trials of the soldiers wife, regard his reserved and silent manners with respect, for though the same sorrows may not darken the sunshine of their lives, their instinct penetrates the recess of the soldiers heart, and the sight of its shattered and wrecked remains often cause a sigh of sorrow, and a tear of commiseration. Let us trust that a merciful God in His divine wisdom, may alleviate the poignant grief of the soldier, and restore him to that happiness he once possessed.

And now kind reader, we bid you a last farewell; but ere the pages of this book are closed, let us speak a word to you, for those unfortunates who abandon their homes on the approach of the enemy to seek refuge in the Confederate lines. Many—alas! too many of its citizens consider the term "refugee" synonymous with that of "*beggar.*" In this idea we err. It is true they are in many instances, reduced to penury, but in their poverty are as different from the mendicant as the good are from the bad. Many of these refugees have lost their homes, their wealth—their everything to retain their patriotism and honor. Some of them adorned the most polished circles in their midst, and many held an enviable position in the State of their nativity or residence. For their country, for our country, for your country, the brave abandoned all they possessed, preferring to live in want among the people of the South, than to revel in luxuries in the midst of our enemies. Seek these exiles. Look upon them as suffering Confederates, and extend the hand of friendship and assistance to all who are in need. Let the soldier know that his wife and children are provided for by you. It will cheer him while in camp, it will inspire him in battle, and if he falls by the hand of the enemy, the knowledge that those he loves will be cared for, will lighten the pangs of Death, and he will die, happy in the thought of falling for his country. Oh! kind reader, turn your ear to the moaning of the soldier's wife—the cries of his children, and let your heart throb with kindness and sympathy for their sufferings. Relieve their wants, alleviate their pains, and earn for yourself a brighter reward than gold or influence can purchase—the eternal gratitude of the defenders of our liberties.

Farewell! if a single tear of sorrow, steals unhidden down your cheek at the perusal of this sad tale—if in your heart a single chord of pity is touched at its recital—we shall have been fully rewarded for the time and labor expended by us. And if at some future day you hear of some soldier's family suffering; sympathise with their afflictions and cheerfully aid in ameliorating their condition, by giving a single thought of "THE TRIALS OF THE SOLDIER'S WIFE."

FINIS.

APPENDIX

In presenting a work of this nature to the reader, the Author takes the opportunity of making an apology for the errors, typographical and otherwise, which may be found therein. The difficulties under which he labored in procuring the publication of the book at this time, when the principal publishers of the South are so busily engaged in publishing works written in foreign parts, and which cost them nothing but the expense of publication, and the procuring of them through our blockaded ports. The book which our readers have just completed perusing, is filled with many errors; too many, in fact, for any literary work to contain. The excuse of the Author for these, is, that at the time the book was in press he was with the Army of Tennessee performing his duties, which prevented him from reading the proof sheets and correcting all mistakes which crept in during composition. The party on whom devolved the duty of reading the proof performed his work as well as could be expected, for, in some instances, the errors were the fault of the Author, and not that of the printer, who labored under many disadvantages in deciphering the manuscript copy of the book; the greater part of which was written on the battle-field, and under fire of the enemy. It is thus that in the first page we find an error of the most glaring character possible, but which might have been the Author's, as well as the printer's omission. Thus, the Author is made to say that the "aristocracy" of New Orleans were "well known by that elegance and etiquette which distinguish the *parvenu* of society." Now the intention, as well as the words of the author, represented the "aristocracy" in quite a different light. That line should have read "that elegance and etiquette which distinguish *the well-bred* from the *parvenu* of society, etc." Nevertheless, the whole sense of the sentence is destroyed by the omission of the *italicised* words, and the reader is left to infer that the aristocracy of New Orleans are the *parvenu* of society; rather, we must admit, a doubtful compliment, and quite in accordance with the following words, which go on to speak of "the vulgar but wealthy class of citizens with which this country is infested." Now we do not pretend for a moment to believe that our readers would imagine that we meant the sentence quoted in the sense it appears, and they may, perhaps, pass it over without noticing the errors complained of; but when such errors should not exist they become a source of much annoyance to the author, and could they have been rectified before it was too late, they should never have appeared in print. In fact, after discovering that an error of so gross a nature existed in the first pages of the book, the author would have had the entire "form" reprinted, had not the extravagant price of paper, and its great scarcity, precluded the possibility of such an idea being carried into effect. The errors, therefore, remain, and for them we would claim indulgence, although readily admitting that none is deserved.

And now we desire to say a few words relative to the work you have just completed reading. It may appear to you a wild and extravagant tale of hardships and privations which existed only in the imagination of the author. Were your supposition correct, we should rejoice, but unfortunately, every day brings us scenes of poverty that this work lacks in ability to portray, in sufficient force, the terrible sufferings borne by thousands of our people. In the plenitude of our wealth, we think not of poor, and thus we cannot tell or find out the hundreds of poverty stricken wretches who cover the country. Our natures may be charitable even, but we only give charity where it is asked for, and await the coming of the mendicant before our purses are opened. By these means alone do we judge the extent of suffering in the land, and, not hearing of many cases of penury, or receiving many applications for assistance, we believe that the assertions of great want being among the people are untrue, and we purposely avoid searching for the truth of such assertions. The design of the author, in this little book, has been to open the eyes of the people to the truth. If he has painted the trials of the soldiers wife more highly colored than reality could permit, it has been because he desired to present his argument with greater force than he could otherwise have done; and yet, if we examine well the picture he presents; take it in its every part, and look on each one, we will find that it does not exaggerate a single woe. We have seen far greater scenes of wretchedness than those narrated herein; scenes which defy description; for their character has been so horrible that to depict it, a pen mightier than a Bulwer's or a Scott's would be necessary.

The tale which the reader has just finished perusing is taken from scenes that *actually occurred* during the present war—except, perhaps, that part which relates the tearing of the mother from the bedside of her dead child. In every other respect all that is narrated in the foregoing pages are strictly true, and there are parties now in the South, who, when they read this work, will recognize in themselves, some of the characters represented herein. The Author would rejoice, for the sake of humanity and civilization if the tale he has written was only a fiction of his own imagining; but did it not contain truths the work would never have been written. No other object than that of calling attention to the vast misery and wretchedness which at the present time of writing abounds in the South, prompted the Author to pen the pages which you have perused. He has witnessed them himself; he has seen the soldiers wife absolutely starving, and from a slender purse has himself endeavored to relieve their necessities. To present before the world the fact that there are thousands in our midst who are in *absolute beggary*, has been the object of the writer, and to call on those who are able to do so, to aid these unfortunates, is his purpose. This book is an appeal to the Rich in favor of the Poor. It is the voice of Humanity calling upon Wealth to rise from her sluggish torpor and wrest the hungry and threadbare victim from the grasp of Famine, and drive desolation from our midst. If this call is answered; if the wealthy awake to their duty and save the wretched beings who are in our midst, then the Author will have gained a richer reward than all the profits accruing from this work. He will have been more than rewarded by the knowledge that he has been the instrument, through which charity has once more visited the South, and swept oppression and want from our land. Such scenes as those we daily witness were never seen, even in the mildest form a few short years ago. Prior to the war there was scarcely a beggar in the South, and from one end of the country to the other could we walk without hearing the voice of the mendicant appealing to our benevolence. How changed now! In every city of the South the streets are filled with ragged boys and girls stopping each passer by and asking aid. It is a disgrace to humanity and to God, and that such things should be in our land, whose sons have exhibited such heroism and devotion.—Many of these beggary are the sons and daughters of our soldiers—of our honored dead and heroic living. To the soldier who lies beneath the sod a martyr to his country's cause, their sufferings are unknown; but if in Heaven he can witness their penury, his soul must rest ill at peace and weep for those on earth. To the soldier, who is still alive and struggling for our independence, the letter that brings him news of his wife's and children's poverty must bring him discontent, and render him unwilling to longer remain in the army and struggle for liberty while they are starving. How many times have not desertion taken place through this very cause. In Mississippi we witnessed the execution of a soldier for the crime of desertion. On the morning of his execution he informed the minister that he never deserted until repeated letters from his wife informed him of her wretched condition; informed him that herself and her children were absolutely starving. He could no longer remain in the army; the dictates of his own heart; the promptings of his affection triumphed and in an evil hour he deserted and returned home to find her tale, alas! too true. He was arrested, courtmartialed and *shot*. He had forfeited his life by his desertion and bore his fate manfully; his only fear being for the future welfare of that wife and her children for whom he had lost his life. When he fell, pierced by the bullets of his comrades, was there not a murder committed? There was, but not by the men who sentenced him to death. They but performed duty, and, we are charitable enough to suppose, performed it with regret. The murderers were the heartless men who are scattered over the land like, locusts, speculating on the necessities of the people, and their aiders and abettors are those who calmly sat with folded arms, and essayed not to aid his family. Rise, O my readers and aid the poor of our land. Let your hearts be filled with mercy to the unfortunate. Remember that

"The quality of mercy is not strain'd It droppeth, as the gentle rain from heaven Upon the place beneath; it is twice blessed, It blesseth him that gives and him that takes: 'Tis mightiest in the mightiest; it becomes The crowned monarch better than his crown:"

and in performing an act of charity you bless yourself as well as the one who is benefited by such charity.

We shall now close our remarks with the hope that the reader will appreciate the motive which prompted the writing of this book. As will be seen, it has no plot—it never was intended to have any. The Author intended merely to write a simple narrative when he commenced this work, and to place before the public in the most agreeable form of reading, a subject of vital importance to the Confederacy, and to impress upon the minds of the wealthy their duty to the poor. He knows not whether he has succeeded in the latter hope, and he could have wished that some other pen had taken up the subject and woven it into a tale that could have had a better and more lasting effect than the foregoing is likely to have. Nevertheless he trusts that all his labor is not lost, but that some attention will be paid to his words and a kinder feeling be manifested towards refugees and the poor than has hitherto been shown. If this be done then nothing but the happiest results can follow, and the blessings of thousands, the heartfelt blessings of thousands on earth, will follow those who aid in the work of charity, called for by the present emergency, and from the celestial realms the voice of God will be heard thanking His children on earth for their kindness to their fellow mortals.

For the publication of this work the Author has to thank the kind proprietor of the "Atlanta Intelligencer," Col. Jared I. Whitaker. To this gentleman is he indebted for being able to present the work to the public, and to him does the Author extend his sincere thanks. In Col. Whitaker the Confederacy has one son who, uncontaminated by the vile weeds of mortality which infest us, still remains pure and undefiled, and, not only the obligations due from the author are hereby acknowledged, but as one who has witnessed the whole souled charity of this gentleman, we can record of him the possession of a heart, unswayed by a sordid motive. To this gentleman are the thanks of the author tendered, with the wish that he may live many long years to reap the reward due to those, who, like himself, are ever foremost in deeds of charity and benevolence.

END OF APPENDIX

Milton Keynes UK
Ingram Content Group UK Ltd.
UKHW030741071024
449371UK00006B/675

9 789362 095374